IF YOU CAN'T
CALM THE WATERS,
LEARN TO
RIDE THE WAVES

How to Succeed in Turbulent Times

IF YOU CAN'T CALM THE WATERS, LEARN TO RIDE THE WAVES

Clifton Anthony McKnight

© 2010, 2012 Quantum Success Systems, All rights Reserved

All rights reserved. This book may not be reproduced in whole or in part, stored in a retrieval system, or transmitted in any form or by any means electronic, mechanical, or other without written permission from the publisher, except by a reviewer, who may quote brief passages in a review.

How to Succeed in Turbulent Times

IF YOU CAN'T CALM THE WATERS, LEARN TO RIDE THE WAVES

Clifton Anthony McKnight

This book is dedicated to my Maker, my family and friends at home and work who stand with me when times are hardest and to you-- with the hope that it can help you ride the tide or stand against it when necessary. You do make a difference.

Updated and reformatted, September, 2012.

How to Succeed in Turbulent Times

IF YOU CAN'T CALM THE WATERS, LEARN TO RIDE THE WAVES

Clifton Anthony McKnight

Set out to make a difference. God will back you up.

Table of Contents:

Introduction ...8

How to Use this Book

Chapter One ...10
Let's Frame This

A Rewrite before the First Printing?? ✳ Sometimes We Have To "Reboot" ✳ A Shift in Mindset, Know Thyself - A Catalyst for Quantum Leaps ✳ **Interview – Dr. Mark Holland** ✳ Wave at the **STAR** - **S**ayings, Thoughts, Actions, **and References**

Chapter Two ...27
The Success Wave in Human Nature

Will (Wheel) -Of- Fortune ✳ Quantum Success The Source ✳ Attitudes, Thoughts, Beliefs, and Values ✳ Actions ✳ Effects, Outcomes, (Circumstances), Consequences ✳ Successes ✳ Selected Memory ✳ And The Cycle Continues ✳ A Word Of Caution ✳ **Interview - George Jefferson** ✳ Wave At The **STAR** - Sayings, Thoughts, Actions, References

Chapter Three ...49
Cultivating the Mind for Success (Tapping In)

How to Succeed in Turbulent Times

<u>IF YOU CAN'T CALM THE WATERS, LEARN TO RIDE THE WAVES</u>

Clifton Anthony McKnight

Perspective, Action, Reaction ✶ The Wave (Cloak) Called Circumstance ✶ **Interview - Elliott Marbury** ✶ "One man's feast"... ✶ Not Just Why; Why Not? ✶ **STAR**

Chapter Four ...70
Spirit, Mind, Body, Spirit

Remembering the Success Wave ✶ What We Abuse or Do Not Use We Stand to Lose ✶ The Perspiration Wave 1 – Worry, Fear, Hurt, and Pain – and Victory ✶ The Perspiration Wave 2 - Exercise, Practice, the Real Deal ✶ "Being" with Your "Self" (Mind, Body, Spirit) ✶ **Interview – Ruth Norris** ✶ **STAR**

Chapter Five ...95
How to Feel Great About Life (Even in Turbulent Times)

Prayer ✶ Take Inventory - Count Your Blessings Regularly ✶ Unload Your "Sack of Potatoes ✶ " Create a Commercial ✶ Ride with the Tide - Associate with People Who Believe In You ✶ Redress Distress for Success ✶ 101 Ways to Cope With STRESS ✶ People and Prayer for When the Tsunami Comes ✶ **Interview - Sunilda Zabala** ✶ **STAR**

Chapter Six ...116

How to Succeed in Turbulent Times

IF YOU CAN'T CALM THE WATERS, LEARN TO RIDE THE WAVES
Clifton Anthony McKnight

Get a Panoramic View of the Ocean ✷ Help Someone Else Across the River ✷ Make it a Habit, Understand the Value of the Rain – Transmutation and Gleaning Good From All Things ✷ **Interview – Dr. Maureen Edwards** ✷ **STAR**

Chapter Seven . . . 138
Self-direction - Where are You Headed?

View It From the Mountain-Top ✷ Obtain Your Map or Draw it ✷ Learn the Lay of the Land ... and Sea (See) ✷ Choose Your Vessel ✷ Test the Waters – Often ✷ Set Your Course ✷ Set Your Sails (Self-programming) ✷ **Interview - Dr. Mary McKnight-Taylor** ✷ **STAR**

Chapter Eight . . . 152
Getting Others Involved With Your Success

Even before You Go to "Sea" (See), You Can Begin to Make Your Net Work (Network) ✷ Help Paddle Someone Else's Boat ✷ Think Bridges ✷ **Interview – Michael Thomas** ✷ **STAR**

Chapter Nine . . . 168
Prosperity, the Beginning

Cultivating "Prosperity Consciousness" ✷ Finances, Oceans, Sunshine , and Rain - The Inner Self and Other Gifts that Money Can't Buy ✷ Build a Better Tomorrow, Today ✷ **"Interview"** – Bob Parsons

How to Succeed in Turbulent Times

IF YOU CAN'T CALM THE WATERS, LEARN TO RIDE THE WAVES

Clifton Anthony McKnight

STAR

Acknowledgements ...189

About The Author ...198

How to Succeed in Turbulent Times

IF YOU CAN'T CALM THE WATERS, LEARN TO RIDE THE WAVES

Clifton Anthony McKnight

Introduction

"How one proceeds has more to do with one's perspective than with one's circumstances"- Clifton McKnight

How to Use this Book

The short answer as to "how to use this book" is similar to the answer to a riddle, "Where does an 800 pound gorilla sit?" **Answer**: "Anywhere it wants to." This section offers some possibilities for your consideration for creating value in your interaction with this book. One way to do this is to point out the resources and strategies built into the design.

You can use it as a workbook. The book introduces suggested actions at the end of each chapter that can readily be part of a curriculum. Your focus on activity and solution can provide a positive environment for managing life's challenges.

Depending upon when you are reading this, there may be valuable updates, tools, and resources at the website, www.motivision.net or www.cliftonmcknight.wordpress.com that you may find quite useful as well.

I have written this book hoping that as you read it, you will harmonize with the concepts presented. In

IF YOU CAN'T CALM THE WATERS, LEARN TO RIDE THE WAVES
Clifton Anthony McKnight

engaging the material, you will be better positioned to apply many of the ideas and strategies for your personal use.

I undoubtedly break a number of literary rules in this written communication to you. Throughout the book, I move from "I" to "we" to "you," to "he" and from "he" to "she." I will speak in past, present, and future tense but always without pretense. Don't waste time searching for what you cannot use--you won't use it anyway. Look for what you can and will use and if it does not perfectly match your needs now, it will be there for you later.

If reading the entire book is more than you intend to do right now, then simply give your attention to the **STAR** at the end of each chapter. I am confident that doing so will produce tasty fruits for your enjoyment and advancement.

So skim, read cover to cover, DO the **STAR,** discuss with someone else, jump around from page to page or do all of the above. You can choose the level of value you want to glean from this book and as you will see, through life's various experiences.

IF YOU CAN'T CALM THE WATERS, LEARN TO RIDE THE WAVES

Clifton Anthony McKnight

Chapter One

Let's Frame This

"We have the power to define our experience; indeed, that is what we do." – *Clif McKnight*

Maybe you should pause for a moment, just for a moment. With all that you have been through, how is it that <u>you</u> are "still standing?" You've been knocked down before, yet you got up and kept on going. You've taken in a little water and choked a bit. You've caught your breath, regained your composure and continued sailing. You've already survived choppy waters. Ask the right questions and you will get the right answers.

We all enjoy smooth sailing in life. Peaceful times are truly to be cherished. However, we find that life often seems to be filled with twists and turns, flows and ebbs and ups and downs. Hey, a little turbulence can sometimes provide a sense of adventure. But when the waves are too high, the sky is too ominous or life takes a down turn for *too long,* we often become distraught and distressed. We desire safe ground and calm waters.

IF YOU CAN'T CALM THE WATERS, LEARN TO RIDE THE WAVES

Clifton Anthony McKnight

For many individuals, it seems that these are extremely stressful times. We find ourselves in struggle mode rather than being at ease or peaceful, with little time for fun. Duress may not be ever-present, but sometimes it sure seems that way. Regardless of how it really is, there appears to be a layer of fear, stress and doubt. People often wonder, "Can I make it through this?" or "Why me???" We sometimes even make the outright assertion, "I can't take this!" Well, the truth is, YES YOU CAN!

Yes, you can go on to realize that there are gifts to be gleaned, lessons to be learned and resources available that might not have been had there been no struggle.. Recognition of this may not soften the blow or even make sense of the struggle. It serves only to transmute tragedy so that even in defeat, we can find meaning and value.

You are the ancestors of others who have been through difficult times and survived--even thrived before you. You are the offspring of individuals who persevered through trepidation, trials and tribulations. Not only can you make it, it is your legacy. You can emerge VICTORIOUS! Read on and prove it to yourself. I contend that you will agree that the stuff of which you are made destines you to accomplish great things in your ever-evolving world. YOUR WORLD is represented by your own interpretations of your experiences and your close relationships.

You may have read or heard that "it rains upon the just and the unjust." It follows that "stuff happens" to the prepared and to the unprepared as well. It just seems to

IF YOU CAN'T CALM THE WATERS, LEARN TO RIDE THE WAVES
Clifton Anthony McKnight

be different "stuff." Moreover, it is how differently we interpret and respond to the *same* stuff that makes the difference.

Regardless as to what your situation is at the moment--be it positive or painful, if you will but relate to the moment, even down the road, you can reap its lessons.

A Rewrite before the First Printing?

"Life comes at you fast!" a television commercial chimes. Indeed, far too often we find ourselves blindsided by the trials and tribulations of life. Life is constantly evolving but you can succeed--you can make it and with the right perspective, you can use trials and tribulations to make a better and more complete you! I had all but completed this book albeit internally, when life's twists and turns found me on my rumpus, dazed and unstable. What was I to do, and how was I to make it through?

As I am affiliated with the mental health field, I regularly strive to help others maintain their footing in life. However, I found myself uncharacteristically off balance far longer than I expected. Even as this work is being penned, I remain in a state of recovery and rediscovery. Writing or journaling can be a great tool for navigating troubled waters. After all, new challenges, problems and crises sometimes arise even while critical issues are being managed.

How to Succeed in Turbulent Times

IF YOU CAN'T CALM THE WATERS, LEARN TO RIDE THE WAVES
Clifton Anthony McKnight

Isn't that what it is all about? As Donnie McClurkin, gospel performer and producer sang with his choir in a song I heard on the radio, "We fall down, but we get up!" This revised 1st edition is for those of you who struggle personally yet strive to still reach out to help others. You continue to make a difference and if you stay the course, invariably you will be better equipped for the next wave.

Sometimes we have to "reboot."

These days, most people are familiar with the computer repair concept of "restart and reset." The computer freezes and appears to be broken. Or perhaps your printer does not respond or the modem does not seem to be functioning properly. You turn everything off, wait a few seconds and turn everything on again. Sometimes when things in your life seem totally off track and you grow weary, you just need to take a few moments or a few days to reboot.

You now have this resource in your hands. You are not merely reading when your eyes flow over the words and messages in this book. You are internally processing this reading experience. Allow yourself to get the most from this experience by finding the catalysts to stimulate YOURSELF from within.

Observe how experiences noted in this book make you feel or remind you of your personal experiences. Make it a priority to give YOURSELF space to explore the lessons, meanings or pathways that follow as a result of

IF YOU CAN'T CALM THE WATERS, LEARN TO RIDE THE WAVES
Clifton Anthony McKnight

your introspection. Consider reaching out to others while reaching in to your highest, most accepting self.

When a negative thought comes your way, simply recognize it as a healthy consideration and appreciate that you are only at a starting point. Other possibilities must exist. If you feel "minus ten," then there must be a "minus nine" and even a "plus ten" out there. After all, you wouldn't be reading this book if you weren't considering the distinct possibility that you just might discover useful information to help yourself or someone else that is in the midst of adversity live better.

You might be saying to yourself, "Another book about how to succeed? AND to succeed when stuff is rough of all times... Oh, COME ON! And yet here I am, reading... and even the author admits to getting knocked to his knees." Well, find yourself a mirror and give yourself a wink. You are poised for transformation.

The Mind, more accurately, the Spirit, will only absorb so much and be asked to endure so much before it is inspired to respond, to take ACTION. And there is no doubt that the natural byproduct of right thinking, of asking the right questions, is right action. It follows the belief that the byproduct of right action is right living.

So, why this book and why now? First, appreciate the idea that nothing occurs that cannot be transmuted into possibility. You are reading this book perhaps because it is your time to shine. Or perhaps you are in the midst of struggle and you could use some information and inspiration. Maybe you are looking for that final push to move yourself beyond the light at the end of the

How to Succeed in Turbulent Times

IF YOU CAN'T CALM THE WATERS, LEARN TO RIDE THE WAVES
Clifton Anthony McKnight

tunnel. Perhaps you are just a good friend checking out this book with someone else in mind, just to be certain that it is useful. This is a noble sentiment; however, be careful not to overlook the benefit it might offer you.

If you have read other books or heard other literary works through technology and found them useful or perhaps just listened to someone offer insights and perspectives that have been of value in the past, it may have prompted you to pick this book up. WHATEVER THE REASON, the timing is right. You can drink deeply, reading each word page by page or you might choose to skim through it first. There is great value in establishing the framework in which to travel.

Check out the table of contents. Review the **STAR** at the end of each chapter. STAR is an acronym for **S**ayings, **T**houghts, **A**ctions **and R**esources. Sound bytes- those mini thoughts or phrases that provide a message with a punch, can be more than enough to justify the time you invest embarking on this journey.

Open yourself to many possibilities. If you expect to find inspiration and insight, you undoubtedly will. You will because you did your part. You will have brought with you a conscious state of readiness. And that makes **ALL** the difference. Congratulations. Make ready; let's go.

A Shift in Mindset

I was doing something completely unrelated to the great goal of writing this book. Suddenly the inspiration

IF YOU CAN'T CALM THE WATERS, LEARN TO RIDE THE WAVES
Clifton Anthony McKnight

seemed to come out of nowhere. It hit me like a ton of bricks, like a huge wave one might say and I thought, "Just let it flow! You can do it. You can *be* it. You do not have to force it...It is already yours! "

I sat down and simply allowed the words to flow onto the paper. By following this process, a great deal more began to happen. Sometimes we get too caught up trying to get things *just right* and wind up not getting it done or taking no action at all.

"Stop trying to doggedly push to write this book; to *"do the thing right*, I thought. Just let it flow. Position yourself. Get up and sit in front of the computer and begin. Before you know it, you will be on a roll."

Consider adapting this sentiment and you may begin to experience a higher level of well-being and accomplishment right out of the starting gate. Go with the flow and breathe life into your true desires. I recall the passage, "*Give it your heart and you give it wings, you give it life."* When you give it your heart and <u>let</u> your dreams take hold, they will blossom from the rich soil (soul) of your being.

We don't have to try to sound a certain way or do things a certain way. Just be yourself, your higher, better, more natural self. If you need to develop a skill or learn something in depth, give it your heart. Don't believe you have enough time? Just fifteen minutes a day, over time, dedicated to a single impassioned thought can create expertise in any area. It can facilitate accomplishment in any effort. Sometimes the time will move so quickly that

How to Succeed in Turbulent Times

IF YOU CAN'T CALM THE WATERS, LEARN TO RIDE THE WAVES
Clifton Anthony McKnight

you find yourself investing more time. You will have gone into a zone.

Know "Thy Selves "- A Catalyst for Quantum Leaps

Each of us has many selves. There is a physical self and a spiritual self. These selves are not independent entities but interdependent parts of your being, parts of the "whole" of "self." Your spiritual self experiences life through your physical self and your physical self has the potential to affect the experiences of your spiritual self. How are your spirits when you are fatigued? Does it not depend on why you are fatigued? How is your spirit affected? By being aware of and in tune with our spiritual self, we connect with the blessings our Maker has in store for us. Some might simply say that we connect with our potential. We may then only begin to understand our purpose and understand that we are never alone, never really, on our own.

Physically, each individual is part of a greater whole. We are like cells of the human body, each with a unique intelligence and responsibility to function as part of something larger than ourselves. We, as independent organisms, become part of an organization or society which functions intelligently based on agreements called laws, mores, and commitments.

Further, each of us is made up of many other selves. We have a thinking self and a feeling self. We also have a private self and a public self.

IF YOU CAN'T CALM THE WATERS, LEARN TO RIDE THE WAVES

Clifton Anthony McKnight

The complex makeup of our reality and society filters our life experience. What we *think* about an experience *defines* that experience and what we immediately *feel* in a given circumstance often results in an automatic response.

Sometimes we attempt to establish a hierarchy of "Selves." Some claim that it is the thinking self that separates humankind from animals and from primitive, instinctive Homo sapiens. Thinking is tantamount to creating. Feeling has been somewhat perceived as an obstacle to overcome, a baser instinct. Yet feeling reflects the experience of thought. It offers *meaning*. Feeling is our connection, bridging spiritual thought to material and vice versa. A material object can stimulate spiritual thought. Sometimes we just need to be still and be in touch with our selves.

To know one's self is to understand our connectedness to one another; and to love one's self, truly, is to love all there is. Conversely, to love another is to honor (and love) the Self. As our native brothers and sisters say in the Lakota tongue, "Mitakuye Oyasin." According to a book with the same title, Mitakuye Oyasin, loosely translated means, "We are all related." A friend who is of the Lakota Sioux explained Mitakuye Oyasin as meaning, "All My Relations including the birds and the animals and the trees. We are ALL one in and with the Great Spirit."

I contend that we are far more than our physical bodies. Long after the body falls away, we are. To understand this concept is to offer greater perspective.

How to Succeed in Turbulent Times

IF YOU CAN'T CALM THE WATERS, LEARN TO RIDE THE WAVES

Clifton Anthony McKnight

Consider the term Atonement. <u>The American Heritage Dictionary</u> defines "atonement" as "amends or reparation made for an injury or wrong."
"Atonement" with a capital "A" is defined as "Reconciliation between God and humankind."

View the varied breakdowns of the word and you will see "To reconcile or harmonize," to be "**At One.**" What does this mean to you? Think about it. We will revisit this further later. When one chooses harmony, discord is transformed and order grows out of chaos.

By being aware of our interconnectedness, we develop an appreciation for doing well on behalf of others as they are but an extension of ourselves. We tap into our true potential. Everything is an extension of us; therefore, every *thing* conceivably may be *influenced* by us.

Spiritually, we have insight far beyond our understanding and as we strengthen our relationship with the Infinite, it brings creativity to us. We are, in essence, the creators of our experiences during this life. Wait... I am not suggesting that we fashion floods, earthquakes, or whether someone or something connives to oppress or victimize us. I am suggesting that we automatically fashion or assign our own interpretations of our experiences, our circumstances, and then choose our responses to those interpretations.

We do not always create what happens to us; we create *how we experience and respond* to what happens to us. Have you ever recalled two people who've had the same experience but different perspectives on it? One may have called it the event that changed her life and filled it

IF YOU CAN'T CALM THE WATERS, LEARN TO RIDE THE WAVES

Clifton Anthony McKnight

with splendor. However, the other viewed it as the beginning of the end. Whether it is losing a job or hitting the Lotto, we have the power to define its impact. We determine how we are going to be as a result of the experience. Note how tragedy was transmuted into triumph in the life of Mark Holland.

I met Mark Holland when he was a student and I was an administrator at Coppin State (CS) University, at that time CS College in Baltimore Maryland. Though more than a decade separates our ages, I consider him as one of my closest friends. In my opinion, Mark has been successful at everything he persistently set out to accomplish. He graduated from Hampton University in Hampton, Virginia. He served as an officer in the military. He has had success as an engineer, real estate investor and even a pastor, acquiring a Doctorate of Divinity. Below is a summary of our conversation.

Interview - Mark Holland D.Min.

> *Mark:* I have to say, Clif that I have managed to navigate my ups and downs in life fairly well. I am not saying it has been a walk in the park. I have experienced the same disappointments and life issues that we all face from time to time. I will be brief, for as you know, generally I am a private person, so what I am about to tell you is not easily shared.
>
> I think the greatest challenge of my life to date occurred for me when my sister took her own life. She had a long battle with severe depression. When it happened,

How to Succeed in Turbulent Times

IF YOU CAN'T CALM THE WATERS, LEARN TO RIDE THE WAVES
Clifton Anthony McKnight

I was staggered to my core. My faith was sorely tested and I entered a deep depression myself.

It took some time before I would see the light of day. Time, pain, solitude and grief preceded prayer and ultimately a fairly major shift in my life. Kim's death taught me to cherish the moment and to not waste precious life worrying. Of course, we all have worries, but I work to focus on what I can do today to make at least my world better.

Clif: Please elaborate on what you mean when you say "my world."

Mark: I refer to my relationship with God, my life experience, to my family and to all the people in my life, the people that my existence touches. I can make the greatest difference in "my world." When you think about it, for each of us, "my world" can signify something different. For me, my family, my congregation, my friends, my tenants, and my coworkers, the people I interact with professionally and those I come into contact with as I go about my daily business make up my world. This can amount to hundreds of people. Add the people who listen to my tapes or come to hear me speak and you may have thousands to count. The closer I get to the core of my world, the deeper the focus and intensity to serve.

Now, it is important that you don't misunderstand me here. Life is so fragile that it would be a mistake for me to continue worrying about making everyone else

IF YOU CAN'T CALM THE WATERS, LEARN TO RIDE THE WAVES
Clifton Anthony McKnight

happy, even in my world. I have come to recognize that if I am going to be true to my life, to my calling, I had best be conscious of and a good steward of what keeps me happy. In order to manage "my world" and all its twists and turns, I had better focus on my joy and minimize if not eliminate the frets, burdens, and worries that others would gladly put on my shoulders. If I am not joyful, how can I give it to others?

Clif: And what of connection and extending a hand to others?

Mark: Clif, without a doubt we are more and life is better when we are in service. Paramount to my point is "Seek ye first, the Kingdom of God." Our church name is KINGDOM FIRST MINISTRIES. Seek to know God, seek to know yourself. Be true to that *first*. If you let your vehicle fall apart because you are too busy transporting everyone else, sooner or later, nobody rides.

Clif: I think that says it all, my friend. Thank you.

We can find or create purpose and value out of circumstance or fall prey and be victimized by circumstance. Each choice has an effect, which fuels future perspectives and attitudes. These perspectives or attitudes in turn, influence our future actions, producing results that reinforce our perspectives and continues the cycle.

How to Succeed in Turbulent Times

IF YOU CAN'T CALM THE WATERS, LEARN TO RIDE THE WAVES

Clifton Anthony McKnight

Mark gleaned the gift of the moment, of priority and taking responsibility for one's own happiness. Choose your paradigm. The paradigm we construct perpetually becomes a wheel of fortune or a wheel of misfortune, based on the direction of our will, until we make a change. I call it a "Will of Fortune," appropriately coined by a participant in a leadership "actionshop" I facilitated years ago. (Thank you, Sonya.)

Regardless as to whether you think you can or can't do something, either way, you are right. We so often focus on what hasn't worked and what does not work instead of what *has* worked. What has occurred in your life that has been right, been good? What have you done to benefit yourself or those you love? Don't skim past this. Sit with it. Struggle to get in the space if you have to (You really don't. Just take a few genuinely deep breaths and **let** yourself see.)

Hey, check you out! You are still reading! That is a WHOLE LOT more than what thousands of others are doing. Many people don't take the time to read or reflect for the benefit of others. Some don't carry the temperament or inclination to even reflect on the possible for their own benefit, for that matter. And here you are creating your own *Wave*. Prepare to catch it. You may have heard the saying, "If you pray for rain, take your umbrella." Faith is to be reflected in our actions if it is to bear fruit.

Now let's explore what I call the "Success Wave in Human Nature." You are ready for a closer look at "The Will of Fortune." On the other hand, it may be a good

IF YOU CAN'T CALM THE WATERS, LEARN TO RIDE THE WAVES
Clifton Anthony McKnight

idea to reflect and review what you just read before reading on. It is amazing what kind of insights we have when we give ourselves the opportunity to connect, to let it in and "let it out."

How to Succeed in Turbulent Times

IF YOU CAN'T CALM THE WATERS, LEARN TO RIDE THE WAVES

Clifton Anthony McKnight

Wave at the **STAR** - **S**ayings, **T**houghts, **A**ctions, **R**esources

Sayings

Remember, "It's all relative."

"Give it your heart and you give it wings."- Clif McKnight

"It rains upon the just and the unjust." Paraphrase of Holy Bible, Matthew 5:45

"If you pray for rain, take your umbrella."

Thoughts

You are the offspring of those who persevered through trepidation, trials and tribulations. Not only can you make it, it is your legacy.

Sometimes we have to "restart and reset."

We have the power to define our experience; indeed, that is what we do.

Remember to embrace "Inspirational dissatisfaction." Be grateful yet discontent enough to be inspired to make a difference.

Think you can or think you can't. Either way, you are right.

"Cherish the moment... [Do] not waste precious life worrying." – Mark Holland

How to Succeed in Turbulent Times

IF YOU CAN'T CALM THE WATERS, LEARN TO RIDE THE WAVES

Clifton Anthony McKnight

Creative possibilities emerge as we interpret and respond to the same stuff with anticipation.

Actions

1. List three things you intend to gain while reading this book
2. Note three actions you can take right now to position yourself for maximum benefit. Examples include scheduling time for reading and taking action. Establish a space where you can be the most relaxed and receptive to possibilities and plan to go there. Another example might be to discuss what you are reading with someone else who may or may not be reading or listening to the same book.
3. Begin to expect solutions to issues to present themselves to you. Pick up a folder or binder and label it something like "Possibilities" or "Problem Solving Ideas" or "Problem Blasters."
4. Ask yourself, "How do I reconcile with God?"
5. Revisit the section "Know Thy Selves." Explore your "selves"; write down your thoughts regarding the many dimensions you have. How can you use this insight?

Resources

Prayer, meditation – inner resources
Your spiritual text - Bible, Torah, Quran, Bahai Writings, etc.

Mitakuye Oyasin – Dr. A. C. Ross

How to Succeed in Turbulent Times

IF YOU CAN'T CALM THE WATERS, LEARN TO RIDE THE WAVES
Clifton Anthony McKnight

Chapter Two

The Success Wave in Human Nature

"Thought is the blossom, language the bud, action the fruit behind it." —Ralph Waldo Emerson

When I began developing this model in 1987, it was entitled "Wheel of Fortune," like the game show. " As I view the process as cyclical, constantly reinforcing itself, I thought it quite appropriate and catchy. Eventually, I changed it to Wheel-o-Fortune and later to the Quantum Success Wheel-o-Fortune in honor of the concept of the Quantum Leap.

Over the years, the model has evolved largely through the privilege of interaction with others to the Quantum Success Will of Fortune. The use of "will" is credited to a participant of a leadership and supervisory development workshop for a fine bi-county organization in Maryland called the Maryland National Capital Park and Planning Commission. The participant, Sonya Kitchens, made the rather insightful observation that the model really spoke to the individual "will" and coined the "Will of Fortune." Thank you, Sonya.

IF YOU CAN'T CALM THE WATERS, LEARN TO RIDE THE WAVES

Clifton Anthony McKnight

The model acknowledges our innate hardwiring to perpetuate what we *believe* and *know* to be true in our individual realities. What we believe **is** may as well **be** because we will tend to act as if it were true. We will even produce outcomes, recollect experiences and interpret our present experiences to validate what we believe. As a result, it is most difficult for some people to shift to new situations. The belief that things are as they are have so much (self affirmed) evidence that it is difficult to consider that there may be other possibilities than *those cemented in the belief*.

Quantum Success represents our highest, best selves. It represents our starting point for implementing positive change as it is our connection with our spiritual selves, with God and the universe. Such an overarching connection represents our kinship with one another. Knowing this part of ourselves impels us to engender positive attitudes, thoughts, beliefs and values.

With such a solid foundation of self perception, our actions follow suit, leading to a series of positive outcomes or, at the very least, a positive perspective regarding the outcomes. That is, we are able to see the silver lining in the cloud; we can create lemonade from the lemons of life's experiences. These positive perspectives about our outcomes are channeled to our memory. While everything we experience in life may be recorded in our minds, we tend to recall those things that harmonize with our perspective. I call this "Selected Memory." We file those experiences that reinforce our attitudes, thoughts, beliefs and values into a readily accessible place in our minds. Thus, we are able to reinforce our attitudes, thoughts, beliefs, and values--and the cycle continues.

The  *Will of Fortune*

The Will (Wheel) - Of – Fortune

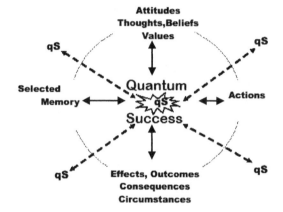

IF YOU CAN'T CALM THE WATERS, LEARN TO RIDE THE WAVES

Clifton Anthony McKnight

Quantum Success, the Source

Quantum Success (qs) is the center of the Will - Of-Fortune. It is the core of life and living. Its definition goes beyond all boundaries and thus connects art, science, philosophy and religion. Here qs represent our connection with the Infinite. It is our spiritual connection, the *Creative Nature* in each of us. Whether we understand *It* or not, *It* is there. Whether we work with *It* or not, *It* will produce.

Within each of us lie resources beyond our comprehension. We are like vessels in a stream of consciousness interrelating with the stream, occasionally melding with it. We are like cups striving to be filled. If we could only see that we are immersed in the spring, filled and surrounded; at one with the waters. To bring it closer into perspective, imagine that the very cup is made of water. It is frozen so that it might be distinguished in shape but nonetheless, it is very much a part of the very water it seeks to capture.

In the Will-o-Fortune, Quantum Success (**qs**) represents our link to the Infinite, our oneness with the universe. Two major precepts for all intentions are representative of Quantum Success: 1] Unlimited Potential (**UP**); and 2] Interconnection. It would be inappropriate to attempt to discuss these two concepts separately as the very essence of qs engages them both. UP can be tapped into through use and recognition of our interconnection.

How to Succeed in Turbulent Times

IF YOU CAN'T CALM THE WATERS, LEARN TO RIDE THE WAVES
Clifton Anthony McKnight

Consider the power and ability one might have that recognizes the connection with a magnificent intelligence or even a community who wants only the best for that one. What splendor and completeness would be experienced with the realization of unconditional love and connection? If we are part of a whole and that whole is represented in every thing, is there any wonder that everything is within our reach?

Look at the model again. FIRST, we settle down. We get in touch with our Highest Self, our connection with the Infinite, the Universe, God, energy, matter, Universal Intelligence, the Essence of all things and the Source of all things. However, if we choose to identify and relate to these concepts, we are more empowered when we embrace our oneness with them.

We know that we all have various capabilities. Imagine our capability when we connect with those around us who vibrate at the same thought frequency. When we connect on an emotional or a spiritual level and share the same vision, the same desires, how much farther can we go?

We also acquire insights from others' experiences through personal contact, observation, reading, watching fiction and non-fiction theatre in all their forms. Most importantly, we have the capacity to *imagine*.

Imagination stimulates and facilitates. Imagination creates. The essence of your individual reality is fostered by your imagination. It also can be used to create or to destroy. Even, misguided, maladaptive minds bear fruit.

IF YOU CAN'T CALM THE WATERS, LEARN TO RIDE THE WAVES

Clifton Anthony McKnight

The fruit may be rotten, poisonous fruit, but it is fruit nonetheless.

When we realize our oneness, misguided thought is dispelled. We have but to still ourselves long enough to love ourselves and recognize our relationship with all that is. We feel in harmony with the rhythm of life.

"The Light of a Single Candle Shows the Way."
- Clif McKnight

As previously noted in our model, *Quantum Success* represents essentially two things-- Interconnectedness and Unlimited Power. Science, Religion and Philosophy have terminologies and concepts which coincide with Quantum Success. They are *Energy, Infinity, Universe,* or *Matter, God* and *Love*. All refer to that one essence from which all else exists. We may need all disciplines to define *It*. What works for me is, God is Love and God's Love is in us. God's Love creates. It is our legacy to create with God's Love.

Once we tap into our innermost resources, into that essence of all things, we begin to understand and more consciously shape our reality. We are clearer about our

IF YOU CAN'T CALM THE WATERS, LEARN TO RIDE THE WAVES

Clifton Anthony McKnight

relationship with one another and with our place in this space. First, we choose our perspective then we shape our reality. We quickly grow to accomplish inconceivable things.

"..The man of today scarcely recognizes the man of yesterday." - Ralph Waldo Emerson

The path to Quantum Success is a personal journey filled with champions and cheerleaders in the form of teachers, coaches, family and friends. At times, we are inspired by a loving touch or a sincere compliment. The path is also filled with challenges. I believe Les Brown, noted author and motivational speaker, say something to the effect of *"Opportunities are challenges cleverly disguised as problems,"* or *"Problems are just opportunities in work clothes."*

Sometimes we can transform a cruel gesture or a scowled glare. Thoughtless acts, deliberate slights, and dismissive remarks need not destroy our equilibrium. Our mindset can transmute the experience into potential motivation.

Recognizing the unlimited capacity that exists within us unleashes powerful resources. As human beings, we have the multi-layered ability to function as transmitter, receiver, programming coordinator and Dee Jay simultaneously. We generate and interpret messages or themes within ourselves. We psychically or experientially affirm these interpretations and we act on them.

How to Succeed in Turbulent Times

IF YOU CAN'T CALM THE WATERS, LEARN TO RIDE THE WAVES

Clifton Anthony McKnight

Filter all that you feel, think, and say, in **Faith, Hope, and Love**. *Thoughts, feelings,* and beliefs become words, deeds, and other manifestations.

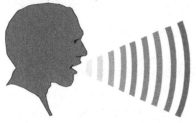

Check your filter for incoming messages. On what wave length are you operating? What channel picks up your interpersonal frequency? Where is your dial tuned? When you are *tuned in,* you will *get* the message. What you send out will also be received in kind. Choose your frequency. Choose carefully the *station* you want to experience.

Attitudes, Thoughts, Beliefs and Values

How to Succeed in Turbulent Times

IF YOU CAN'T CALM THE WATERS, LEARN TO RIDE THE WAVES

Clifton Anthony McKnight

It is more than a stretch to say we can "calm the waters." Water is gonna do what water's gonna do. Having said that, I am using a little literary license with the metaphor *calming the waters* to illustrate a point. We do, in fact, *calm the waters* when we are able to avert a tragedy, diffuse an argument or calm ourselves during a confrontation. We do *"ride the waves"* when we keep on going despite great adversity.

Just as we have the imagination and ability to create a dam through the science of engineering, we have the capacity to forge towards our loftiest goals while holding negativity at bay. To design and build structures such as the Hoover Dam which holds megatons of water seems almost miraculous. How much more miraculous is the persistent existence of life itself? To suggest that we are mere hapless leaves in the cosmic wind is narrow minded and shortsighted at best.

We are far from being helpless ships without a rudder. We have been engineered for success. Look at the process of human growth and development. Consider how children evolve from infant to toddler. Children learn early how to obtain what they want. They observe and mimic those around them as best as they can. Eventually, predictably, they learn to walk and talk.

At first, stepping or even standing is unsteady. Every effort requires support. Because she sees others doing it, she expects, she thinks, she believes that she will walk and talk – and so she does. Proverbs 23:7 of *The Bible* says, "As a man thinks in his heart, so is he." What

IF YOU CAN'T CALM THE WATERS, LEARN TO RIDE THE WAVES

Clifton Anthony McKnight

do you think? What does your Holy text have to say about this?

In a direct sense, attitudes and values stem from thoughts and emotions. I once heard Dave Ellis, then president of an education consulting firm and publishing company and now author of <u>Falling Awake</u> refer to emotion by breaking the word down to Energy in Motion, "E-Motion." It all makes sense. Our emotional state, how we *feel* about ourselves and our environment moves us to ACT!

Actions

While reading this book, suppose you heard a loud thud, followed by a low, growling sound. You pause and consider going into the other room to check things out. As you are debating, into your room jumps a *humongous* nine foot tall, red eyed, sharp toothed, bad breathed, 1,150 pound "**Bearilla." It's not a bear, not a gorilla, but a "*Bearilla*,"** the likes of which you have never seen.

How does your body immediately respond to such a thing? Your heart begins racing. Adrenalin is pumped into your system preparing you for fight or flight...well, in this case flight. Your breathing changes dramatically. You may forget your manners and don't say to the person beside you, "After you," nor would someone likely respond "Oh no, after you" if you did. You become a *different person.*

IF YOU CAN'T CALM THE WATERS, LEARN TO RIDE THE WAVES

Clifton Anthony McKnight

Within a nano second your body changes. The positive consciousness within you says either "Freeze, maybe it'll go away or ...RUN, while you still can!!"

Just before you leapfrog over the person standing between you and the back door, the growl becomes a hearty, almost hysterical laugh. You look over your shoulder without pausing and see that the bearilla head is off and under its arm. A human head protrudes from the shoulders of an apparent cleverly devised costume.

NOW your emotions change again. Your fear becomes relief or perhaps anger, but you immediately again, become someone else...physiologically. Our attitudes and our perceptions both move and limit us. Our perception of danger was enough to change us.

We must be conscious, be awake to what we allow to take root and weed out the negative energy that attempts to take residence in our hearts and minds. We are ready to flow and will move forward when we take the time to understand who we are and what we are about.

My late Aunt Thelma, whom we called "Little T" because my other aunt, her step sister, is also a Thelma ("Big T"), used to refer to those things that seemed to be overwhelming as *Bearillas*.

She also told me of a saying that was scrawled on the walls of a dwelling they called home when they first moved to Baltimore, Maryland many years ago. It read, in graceful dialect, *"Be what you is and not what you ain't. When you ain't what you is, you is what you ain't."* It is time

IF YOU CAN'T CALM THE WATERS, LEARN TO RIDE THE WAVES
Clifton Anthony McKnight

to recognize Our Unlimited Potential and Our Interconnection and "be what we is."

Well, if we take the time, we can all remember times when our perceptions, expectations or trepidation resulted in extreme physiological change, **even when they were not real!** Let this be a glimpse at the power we each possess to create our personal reality and ultimately a synergistic, collective reality....

"I'd like to buy the world a..." If you spent any time in America and watched television for any length of time between the 1970s and 1990s, you know the rest. We have been programmed. By being conscious, by being aware, we can in essence *program* ourselves. At a minimum, we can begin to connect our actions to our purpose.

The actions or inaction we take are directly influenced by our attitudes, thoughts and beliefs. Our actions create. Physicists will confirm that every action has an equal or opposite reaction. Action equals cause; cause begets effect or outcome. There are usually consequences for doing the right thing and also consequences for not doing anything.

Effects, Outcomes, (Circumstances), Consequences, Successes

You haven't seen enough of this "wily willy wheel" yet. We usually obsess about *RESULTS*. Sure, *Results* are critical, *but* PROCESS can be critical, too. Process is the

IF YOU CAN'T CALM THE WATERS, LEARN TO RIDE THE WAVES

Clifton Anthony McKnight

"stuff" of life. I say this because process takes time. Benjamin Franklin is credited as saying, "Dost though love life? Then do not squander time for time is the stuff life is made of."

Examine the model and you will see arrows from that core which represents our Inner self and our connection to the Infinite, our connection with God. We see Attitudes and Thoughts leading to our Actions, and we see the influence of Selected Memory. Closer examination reveals the interrelationship of all the facets, including other persons.

The fundamental principle regarding our capability of succeeding in turbulent times rests with our thoughts and our relationships. The results we seek and the process we use to obtain them are influenced by our thoughts. Moreover, our interpretations of the outcomes in our lives are commensurate to the depth of our personal connection and to our interactions, our limited understanding of the unseen Universe.

A student has a bad experience with mathematics. That student may maintain that he is just not good at mathematics. If he allows that perspective to take root and grow, it becomes "fact" to him. When required to take a mathematics class, he muses, "There is no way I am going to pass this class." He fails the first test. If he passes a test, he may consider it a fluke and otherwise do poorly on homework or quizzes. When the semester ends, lo and behold, the student has failed the class. More accurately, he has *succeeded* at *failing*.

IF YOU CAN'T CALM THE WATERS, LEARN TO RIDE THE WAVES
Clifton Anthony McKnight

Selected Memory

We tend to remember that which supports our perspective. We recall with the slant of our point of view. You may be familiar with the aphorism, "Hindsight is twenty-twenty vision." Well, let me add a "Clif note" or "Clifism": "Hindsight may be twenty- twenty vision, but Insight is golden. "

Negative beliefs attract negative memories and positive beliefs attract positive memories. In fact, the more we think about something, the more we re-experience it. For our memories to be maximally useful, it is helpful to assess its impact and to choose your perspective. The clearer the picture, the easier it is to relegate its place in your database.

The *twenty-twenty vision* of experience is a great teacher. When you go back to examine a past event and how it might have been conducted differently, you benefit from what may have been a previously negative occurrence. You use the twenty-twenty vision of hindsight to conduct yourself in a more prepared manner in order to cope when next such an occasion arises. With your new insight, you are better able to help yourself and someone else who may be faced with a similar experience.

You can also expand your understanding by learning about someone else's experiences. Observe the differences between those who do well and those who don't. Find mentors and involve yourself in mentoring others. Successful people often take an interest in other highly motivated people who pursue a similar journey.

How to Succeed in Turbulent Times

IF YOU CAN'T CALM THE WATERS, LEARN TO RIDE THE WAVES

Clifton Anthony McKnight

Remember, I said, "Hindsight may be twenty-twenty vision," but Insight is golden. As you read, the wisdom in what I have coined Quantum Success may become infinitely clearer. Prayer, introspection, reflection, meditation and planning are activities that lead to insight. In my spiritual framework, to do these things is to "Walk with God."

How does experience help us to continue moving forward when things are most difficult? We notice the challenges that others have faced. We recall experiences we have personally endured. We pray. On coping with illness, death and other hardship, Sandra Glover--nurse, wife, mother and dear friend, suggests that, "We keep going by the grace of God... And seeing others with their crosses to bear and being there for each other. At one point or another, we are all getting tests."

When we have someone around who has gone through similar hardships, it tends to help us manage our own hard times unless our perspective is skewed negatively. When perspective is positive, we have added another memory to support the *"we will get through this"* concept. Having a notion of a God who has seen it all can help us immensely. We can assume that He understands our struggle and we can *remember* this to find comfort.

And the Cycle Continues

Science will support the concept that an object at rest remains at rest and continues moving when in

IF YOU CAN'T CALM THE WATERS, LEARN TO RIDE THE WAVES
Clifton Anthony McKnight

motion. In physics, terms like inertia, resistance and kinetic energy attempt to explain this. To delve more deeply, you might continue with concepts such as space expansion and time differential. However, this concept is beyond the scope of this book. For the purposes of this discussion, let us simply acknowledge the point that an object in motion tends to continue in the direction it is headed until influenced by an outside force.

Borrowing from the physics of matter and space/time makes perfect sense if we consider that "The Process is always the same," as Dave Ellis, author of Becoming A Master Student and Falling Awake said. This tendency is suggested as well in the "Will of Fortune." We tend to more fervently entrench ourselves in what we believe as we attract evidence to support what we believe and the cycle continues, until we interrupt the pattern.

Memories that harmonize with the initial attitudes, thoughts, beliefs and values are more readily accessible to the conscious mind and further perpetuate the perspectives and perceptions we experience. The "wheel" structure of the "Will of Fortune" allows for an attitude or thought to perpetuate itself. Once we embrace a notion, we tend to continue to act on that notion as if it is true. We tend to note and recall experiences that support it.

A Word of Caution

How to Succeed in Turbulent Times

IF YOU CAN'T CALM THE WATERS, LEARN TO RIDE THE WAVES
Clifton Anthony McKnight

It is important to stay conscious of what and how you are affected by things. The "Will of Fortune" can easily be manipulated into a "Will of Misfortune" if one isn't mindful. When we are unclear about our legacy and unaware of our true selves, we can dwell in helplessness and hopelessness, feeling like victims of circumstance unequipped to do anything about it.

Do a search online for the "Karpman Triangle" and you will see many references to this triad of relationships between *Persecutor, Victim and Rescuer*. Noted therapist Dr. *Stephen* B. *Karpman* identified a pattern of interactions that would deem an outside person as the *Rescuer*. All we need to do to empower ourselves is to recognize and invoke the *Rescuer* within. As an extension of ourselves, we can certainly call to others for support but we would be better served to first reach within to address life's challenges. It is key to be inner attentive.

I met George Jefferson while working at Montgomery College. It was immediately clear that George was a high energy, get it done kind of guy with great creativity, plus a wealth of knowledge and experience. Today, among other things, George is Executive Director of The Leadership Academy. Like yours truly, George travels around the country motivating and educating students and professionals alike. He addresses topics on student leadership and getting hired--offering insights from his publications, How To Work With People: BASIC TRAINING for STUDENT LEADERS and DON'T GIVE THEM A REASON TO SAY NO. I have the privilege of sharing his

How to Succeed in Turbulent Times

IF YOU CAN'T CALM THE WATERS, LEARN TO RIDE THE WAVES

Clifton Anthony McKnight

thoughts with you about succeeding in turbulent times. Here is what he had to say.

Interview - George Jefferson

Clif: So, shall I give you the standard questions to stimulate your thinking?

George: I am ready to roll. I know exactly what I would like to share. I keep a piece of paper in my pocket. It is a bit tattered now, but I use it as a reminder of what I can do when I find myself under duress. Below are a few things that I recommend.

1. Life is composed of ups and downs. Don't be discouraged.

2. It is ALWAYS a matter of perspective. When you change the way you look at things, the things you look at change. You see them differently, and that is what changes. Some look at God, and they believe. Then they look at their problem, and they don't.

3. <u>*This,* is not the end.</u>

4. You can encourage yourself. David wrote in the 27th Psalm, "The Lord is my Shepherd…" When you read the entire Psalm, there are moments where he appears to dip out of faith momentarily, and then he stops himself. Carl Jung would say that he is interacting with his Shadow Self. His Stronger self intervened in the direction his weaker self was taking him.

How to Succeed in Turbulent Times

IF YOU CAN'T CALM THE WATERS, LEARN TO RIDE THE WAVES
Clifton Anthony McKnight

5. Things Change...Stick around a minute.

6. Some of the most unlikely people are heroes. David was a shepherd selected to be King over his bigger, stronger, siblings.

7. Being discouraged reduces your strength, reduces your options, saps your strength.

8. Try to go one day at a time and do one thing at a time.

9. A song by Mary Mary called "Yesterday," I have so much heartache and pain in my life but then I DECIDED that yesterday was enough for that.

10. I woke up this morning. I'm cool. ✧

Clearly, George is tuned in to **Quantum Success**. He continues to be energized and inspiring others. For more information about George Jefferson or to book him, visit www.theleadershipacademy.org

IF YOU CAN'T CALM THE WATERS, LEARN TO RIDE THE WAVES

Clifton Anthony McKnight

STAR

Sayings

"Dost thou love life? Then do not squander time, for time is the stuff life is made of." – Benjamin Franklin

"Hindsight may be twenty-twenty vision, but Insight is golden."
-Clifton McKnight

"Thought is the blossom, language the bud, action the fruit behind it." -Ralph Waldo Emerson

"Opportunities are sometimes challenges cleverly disguised as problems." or "Problems are just opportunities in work clothes."
- Les Brown

Thoughts

If you find yourself down in the gutter, as you rise, consider how you got there. That way, you don't have to repeat yourself.

The life we perpetuate is the life we recreate!

Mental begets physical. Persistent or intense thought lead to action and manifestation.

Actions

1. <u>List at least 25 things you know about yourself</u>. Okay, start with *five*. That's **5**... Just don't stop there. Note your strengths and in another column note the areas that

IF YOU CAN'T CALM THE WATERS, LEARN TO RIDE THE WAVES
Clifton Anthony McKnight

need development. Put an asterisk (*) by those characteristics or skills that you know you would rather pay someone else to perform on your behalf than to develop within yourself. Review and expand upon this list regularly.
2. <u>Spend some uninterrupted time with yourself each day.</u> Whether you allocate fifteen minutes or two hours, you will find it to be the most valuable time you will ever invest.
3. Contemplate on the unconditional love of our Maker. Sit with it; experience it. Practice it. You can do this, you know...This is an Action book and you are completing an action chapter. Get in on the ACT. Pause and do this at the next opportunity. Could that be now?
4. If you have been driven to your knees, since you are already down there, say a prayer to help you along your way.

Resources

- World Religions Texts. This time consider cross referencing

<u>As a Man Thinketh</u> - James Allen

<u>As a Woman Thinketh</u> - Dorothy J. Hulst

www.youtube.com –search "What the Bleep"

http://www.scienceface.org/- Layman's Quantum Mechanics

<u>IF YOU CAN'T CALM THE WATERS, LEARN TO RIDE THE WAVES</u>
                    Clifton Anthony McKnight

We Fall Down, But We Get Up! Donnie McLurkin -Song

<u>Falling Awake</u> – David Ellis

<u>http://www.fallingawake.com/</u>

<u>BASIC TRAINING FOR STUDENT LEADERS</u>
                              - George Jefferson

<u>DON'T GIVE THEM A REASON TO SAY NO</u>
                              - George Jefferson

Chapter Three

Cultivating the Mind for Success (Tapping In)

"We become what we think about." – Earl Nightingale

Understanding a little bit about how the mind works can change YOUR life. As indicated in the "Will of Fortune," your evaluations of your thoughts and experiences define your life. It is this assessment that carries you through or takes you down. You calm the waters when you think gently about yourself and others. You calm the waters when your presence of mind and interconnection reach in and reach out to the place in others where peace and love reside.

Cultivating healthy images and perspectives require us to be consciously aware, even vigilant about what we allow to take root in our psyche. To practice harboring positive thoughts for others while thinking kindly of ourselves is an elixir of youth. We tend to feel better when we think positively.

It is also true that we tend to *think* better when we feel better. Wouldn't we be better off thinking and

IF YOU CAN'T CALM THE WATERS, LEARN TO RIDE THE WAVES
Clifton Anthony McKnight

operating through our strengths, from a position of strength? Donald O. Clifton and Marcus Buckingham co-authored a book, and Clifton is reputed to have sparked a movement. The book they co-authored is <u>NOW, DISCOVER YOUR STRENGTHS</u>. The movement is called "Positive Psychology" and "Strengths Psychology."

Donald Clifton was cited by the American Psychological Association as the Father of Strengths Psychology and the Grandfather of Positive Psychology. By focusing on and through your positive attributes, through your preferred styles and tendencies, you can take on the world's challenges and opportunities with poise and competence. Furthermore, this approach will allow you to experience power and confidence and achievement regularly. You are most comfortable and resourceful when you operate from the very center of your strengths and your interpretation of the world takes on a whole new perspective

What a notion! Once we come to know ourselves and thus to know our strengths, the idea is that we can live through those strengths in all of our dealings. Consider this possibility for your life and watch your life's picture change.

Perspective, Action, Reaction

What you see is reflected based upon your vantage point and your frame of reference. Vantage point is tantamount to perspective. Consider a beach ball. Imagine for a moment that you are less than one tenth the

IF YOU CAN'T CALM THE WATERS, LEARN TO RIDE THE WAVES

Clifton Anthony McKnight

size of the ball. Depending on where you stand, assuming that you could only observe one portion or one color of the beach ball at a time, your perspective of the ball may vary significantly. One variance might be where you are in the life cycle. Perspectives vary, priorities vary. Other variances could occur based on financial station, culture, political or social position. Explore various modes and see what you come up with.

How might your vantage point color the perceptions which constitute your reality? Imagine that you are the other person with a different cultural framework and that you are faced with her experiences and her upbringing. Might you see things differently? Would you respond differently to the same situation based on these significantly different life experiences?

Even with the same experiences, people often reach varied conclusions. That is one of the x- factors of being human. We are free to draw individual assessments; to make individual determinations within a mix of group thinking. It is both the experience and the interpretation that matters most.

How to Succeed in Turbulent Times

IF YOU CAN'T CALM THE WATERS, LEARN TO RIDE THE WAVES
Clifton Anthony McKnight

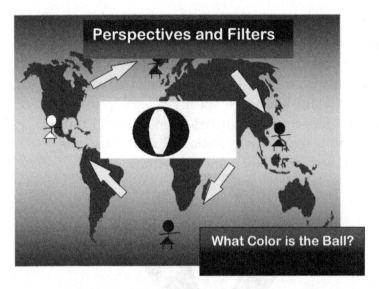

    A worthwhile exercise would be to assess a situation from another person's vantage point. Learn the other person's historical and present day experiences. Write down the other person's life experiences, interpretations, priorities and close associations. Include any observations you may glean.

    Then pretend you are the other person trying to understand your perspective. Try to explain it in writing and read over it a few times. This can provide new insights and help improve understanding, community and harmonious living. You can create win-win when you have depth of appreciation of one another's perspective.

IF YOU CAN'T CALM THE WATERS, LEARN TO RIDE THE WAVES

Clifton Anthony McKnight

It helps to challenge our longstanding beliefs occasionally. By reflecting and objectively evaluating new information as well as our own beliefs, we expand our awareness and can begin to foster a more harmonious existence. We can then greatly improve our personal and global circumstances.

It is particularly valuable to examine perspectives that isolate us from one another. When we examine what isolates us from others within the framework of that which connects us, we can begin to bridge the barriers. When we discover entirely new systems for doing or being, quantum leaps can occur. When someone else operating very differently succeeds, you can learn from that and you can celebrate the observation as well as his success.

When you see someone do well and you understand interconnection, it increases your happiness because part of you made it. When someone is separate

IF YOU CAN'T CALM THE WATERS, LEARN TO RIDE THE WAVES
Clifton Anthony McKnight

and apart, you may experience a feeling of "You have; I don't" and be less enthusiastic about celebrating the other person's success. This usually is not the most productive approach. When you see the connections, you celebrate the success and you say if she can do it, I can too.

Actually, we require one another's success. A motor in and of itself may be a fine thing. Add it to a vehicle and functionality begins. The success of a whole entity relies on the success of its parts. Stay connected. Look to others' success as inspiration and validation that success is within your grasp as well.

Feel your power and effect positive change. Maintaining an awareness of how the things we do interrelate with others and gives us insight into our own influences. We affect ecology; we affect economy. We affect our households, our institutions. We especially affect ourselves.

The Wave (Cloak) Called Circumstance

Some of the circumstances in which we find ourselves are very painful. So valuable is the experience and perhaps even the after effects of these *times of misfortune* when we look beyond the pain. A person loses her job. Unfortunate? Perhaps it is. Perhaps it is not. Usually, loss of work results in short term struggle and long term stress. The key is in our thoughts and in our resultant actions. Where is the lesson and what is the next step?

How to Succeed in Turbulent Times

IF YOU CAN'T CALM THE WATERS, LEARN TO RIDE THE WAVES

Clifton Anthony McKnight

How many times have you heard someone say, "*In retrospect, losing that job was the best thing that could have happened to me* or I never would have been ready for *this* if it hadn't have been for *that*'? Feel the pain, grieve the loss, then **find the good**. Seize the opportunity. Turn a negative into a positive.

I was granted the privilege of interviewing another long-time friend for this book and other publications. I knew that my dear friend was raised largely by his traditional-minded grandfather and was required to work in his grandfather's corner store while his friends played. I know that three men within his closest circle of friends and family are battling serious, life-altering life-threatening, diseases at the time of this writing. I have seen him cope with turbulent work situations and I observe him still striving. Below is a representation of our conversation. It was more than an interview.

Interview - Elliott Marbury

> *Elliott:* What if desperation causes you to give up and you jump off of the top of a 100 story building and halfway down, the idea that could save the day comes into your head?
>
> *Clif:* Great way to start the conversation. You were just saying earlier about challenges in life and how they kind of get us and when we look at where we are today sometimes we...what was your statement?
>
> *Elliott:* We were talking about a quote I had heard, and someone asked me, "If you lost everything you had and

How to Succeed in Turbulent Times

IF YOU CAN'T CALM THE WATERS, LEARN TO RIDE THE WAVES
Clifton Anthony McKnight

then got it back, how would you feel?" Because sometimes we complain so much about where we are in life; because we had something for a long time, it loses its luster. But what if we lost it; then we go crazy. Then suddenly, we get it back. How relieved we become.

It's like losing your wallet. You don't even think about your wallet everyday while you're walking around, or your keys or whatever. Oh, but when it's not there, you know where you think you left it; you begin feeling a state of panic. You look under the seat of your car; you look everywhere.

And then you wonder "Today I went 200 miles away from home. Did I leave it there? Oh no, I don't want to drive back!" You think about all of these things, and your emotions and your body goes through all of these changes. Then all of a sudden, you find it somewhere that you overlooked and you get this great feeling of relief.

Clif: And gratitude.

Elliott: Yes, and gratitude. And it's so funny. As soon as you find it, you go back to your regular routine and you don't think about wallets anymore. And I think it's the same way with that quote. If you lose everything you have, you scramble and try to get stuff and wonder where you're going to sleep at night. So then, you get it back and for a couple of days you're grateful. All of a sudden, things are back to normal.

How to Succeed in Turbulent Times

IF YOU CAN'T CALM THE WATERS, LEARN TO RIDE THE WAVES

Clifton Anthony McKnight

One of the points is that we have to implement gratitude in our daily routine. We need to take some time to just meditate on what we do actually have, whether that's people or things. And the other thing we talked about was how we use the saying, "it's all relative," and sometimes we don't really think about what that really means.

I was relaying to you about the person who had an accident and had to have an operation and how he was at 70% of his former self physically. He had to work on getting back to 100% and lamented the loss. After that, the man had a few setbacks that took him back to about 10%. What he would give to be back at 70% of his wholeness.

I'm just saying each day, wherever we are, we have to learn to appreciate that because though we don't like to **say it,** a lot of times, it could be worse. Well, it could be better too. Yeah, it could be better, but we're working on that. Don't let life have to show you that it could be worse.

Clif: (laughs) So, you don't want a demonstration?

Elliott: No, no. Just accept the fact that it could be worse and just go on and keep looking forward. Try to make it better, but don't be whining and complaining at this point because it could be worse. There are a lot of people out there and all you have to do is look around and know that it is worse for some.

How to Succeed in Turbulent Times

IF YOU CAN'T CALM THE WATERS, LEARN TO RIDE THE WAVES
Clifton Anthony McKnight

You can just look at so many other people's situation and say, "Yeah, it could be worse; you don't have to show me life! I see what worse really is. I am really fine, and I'll take what I have."

Clif: So, here are how the questions are normally asked. I can ask one at a time or you can just do a soliloquy. They are: **What happened? What's happening in your life? How are you; how do you or did you manage? What have you learned? What suggestions do you have for others and what else would you like to say?**

Elliott: Well, let's keep going. The other thing we were talking about was just living life. A comic strip I was looking at was about two animals. The pig was talking to the alligator--I forget exactly what the two animals were. But the pig says, "Hey, what are you doing, Man?" and the alligator answers, "Well, I no longer go to that other church. I now go to the Church of the Gopher," and he's got his head on the ground, listening through the gopher hole, and he says, "This is our preacher, the gopher. He is down here."

The pig says, "Well, when does the gopher ever come up?" And the alligator says, "Oh no, he never comes up out of his hole." Then the pig replies, "Oh, well, it's easy to be some guru gopher when you are living in a hole. Let him come up on the surface and try to deal with people and we'll see how much of a guru he will be." Then he puts his head in the hole and the gopher punches him in the head and knocks him in the air. And the pig says, "Oh, he doesn't like for his sermons to be interrupted."

How to Succeed in Turbulent Times

IF YOU CAN'T CALM THE WATERS, LEARN TO RIDE THE WAVES

                              Clifton Anthony McKnight

The first part was so true; if you're not out there in the real world, it is easy to think you have all your stuff together. You asked what happened with me personally. I can relate. I thought I had it all together. Before I got married, I read my books and I listened to my tapes. Life is just going along and you know, I'm just dealing with the same people at work and this, that and the other.

But in personal relationships, when you have feelings for a spouse and children and all that, if you can keep your head about you when all that is going on, then you have achieved your guru status. Like my brother-in-law said, "Anybody can live life as a monk and give you all the advice in the world on how to survive in the outside world, but when you're in the world and trying to not be of the world, then that is the big challenge in life."

I think that's one of the many things that we work on every day. You may be working on being the best person you can be and not everyone else may necessarily be working on that in that point of their life. We all work at our own level and then all of a sudden, we hook up with somebody at work or any other relationship or whatever, and they aren't working on the same level that we're working on. That's when the real work starts. How do you deal with this situation? How do you handle this situation?

Clif: So, how are you handling this situation?

IF YOU CAN'T CALM THE WATERS, LEARN TO RIDE THE WAVES
Clifton Anthony McKnight

Elliott: Well, the truth is that it's a daily challenge, but I think that's how we actually get better. We actually find out the areas where we need to grow. We may think we have it all together. It's like, "I thought I was over that anger problem!" "I thought I didn't get upset anymore."

But no, you find out you still have some things to work on. I guess if you think about it, if there are no challenges in life, then we don't get to know what we need to work on to get better. So I think challenges can be good. We never ask for those challenges; life figures out how to give them to us anyway.

Clif: So true.

Elliott: We can't get out of here without dealing with those challenges no matter who we are. So I guess that's about it.

Clif: So, how do you manage? You say it's a day by day process. I asked, "What have you learned?" You said that there is always more to do.

Elliott: There is always more to do. You don't get out of this life alive. You don't get out of this life without understanding that you're never totally <u>there</u>. You are always working to understand more… to get "there."

No matter how much you think you have it together, you can't force others along because people have to do

IF YOU CAN'T CALM THE WATERS, LEARN TO RIDE THE WAVES

Clifton Anthony McKnight

it in their own time and place. Stop concerning yourself with what others are doing or not doing. Figure out what things you need to grow and work on. Stop what I like to call "lonely listening" and begin by turning off the TV, the radio and getting all that noise out of your life, even if it's for 15 minutes a day.

Sometimes, you have to be in the quiet and listen and hear what life is trying to tell you because there is always a message there. A lot of times, we hear so much outside noise that we can't hear that *still, small voice* that's trying to give us the direction.

As I get older, I find more and more that the voice is there and the answers come much faster. I think this happens the more we give attention to ourselves. We've all had the experience of thinking about a person and then the next day, he or she calls you or you run into him or her.

Eventually, instead of it happening the next day, it happens the next 5 minutes. As you get more centered and your awareness expands, things manifest more rapidly.

Sometimes, you're not looking for a specific answer, but you happen to think about something as you're driving down the road. Next thing you know, you happen to see just what had run across your mind. Other times, you see things you might not normally have noticed but for the fact that you had just had that certain thought.

How to Succeed in Turbulent Times

IF YOU CAN'T CALM THE WATERS, LEARN TO RIDE THE WAVES
Clifton Anthony McKnight

Whenever you work on something hard enough and long enough, you will begin to attract information from the most unanticipated places. Messages will come, offering you solutions and actions to your task or problem.

Think about how you look at events in your past versus when you were going through the experience. You can better interpret it now very easily, whereas 10 or 20 years ago, you couldn't.
Take time to meditate, pray, grow and observe. That's what I'm talking about more than anything. Take quiet time and observation time.
In your life, you will see that the things that didn't used to mean anything now have meaning. Everything means something and it's just a matter of being in a position to interpret what those things actually mean to you.

Just like when I called you today, we were just having a conversation and you were "of the mind" at that point. Something led you to say, "Hey, let's go ahead and record this." You were at a place to know that you should take advantage of this opportunity right now. That's sort of what I'm talking about.

Clif: Yes, I get it. You also helped me to see another process as opposed to trying to adhere to some predetermined question and answer structure. When it's called for or seems on purpose either to me or you, we may customize our conversation. We are holding a

IF YOU CAN'T CALM THE WATERS, LEARN TO RIDE THE WAVES

Clifton Anthony McKnight

conversation that was intended to be an interview. This way, it is more organic.

Elliott: Yeah, exactly. So, if you learn how to quiet your mind, whatever your eyes are seeing, your mind is then able to put it into whatever you were working on at the time and you don't fight it. The less you fight it, the more that it happens for you. As I'm thinking of all this, this is a part of the front of life. You know, when I was talking about the situation and they were at 70% of their whole, and then they find out they are at 20% and they wish for that 70%?

Clif: Yes.

Elliott: Well, it's that same type of awareness of moment to moment of being aware that where you are is where you are. What is going on where you are may be able to get you where you want to go. It is all about being quiet.

Clif: And in the moment, you can see how it could be quite difficult to get there, but once you get there, you'll be wondering why it was so difficult. Because initially it was like, "I'm at 70% and I remember how great it was at 100%. Oh, what a beautiful time it was. It's not fair." And then things got worse, and you fall to that 20% and you feel like an idiot for wasting the possibilities that were yours at 70%.

How to Succeed in Turbulent Times

IF YOU CAN'T CALM THE WATERS, LEARN TO RIDE THE WAVES
Clifton Anthony McKnight

Elliott: And then you ask, "What were the things at 70% that were beautiful?" You need to ask and figure that out while you're at 70%.

Clif: So that if you get knocked down to that 20% and you learned from the previous lesson, you may pause and say, "Wait a minute, I still have 20%. What can I do and be thankful for now rather than if I was at 3%?"

Elliott: Yes, yes. And I think it is so important to be able to do that.

Clif: And that's worthy to pass on to people if you find yourself in that when you're with someone like that. Thank you.

Elliott: Yes, and it's that old saying, Clif, I was complaining about not having shoes until I saw the man without feet.

Clif: Right, there you go.

Elliott: Hey, we always used to joke about that, "Hey, Man, you don't need any shoes" (laughs).

Clif: (laughs) Yeah, I remember those days, talking about my large rusty *crusties*.

Elliott: If we potentially have feet, then we need to be happy we have feet. But if you don't have feet, that causes a whole lot of other problems.

How to Succeed in Turbulent Times

IF YOU CAN'T CALM THE WATERS, LEARN TO RIDE THE WAVES

Clifton Anthony McKnight

Clif: But if you have no feet, then be thankful that you have legs.

Elliott: Exactly! A lot of people can live like that. And that's a part of the catch 22. We don't want to be *satisfied;* we need to be like Paul in the Bible who said he learned to be content. You are locked up in jail, and you don't want to be there, you're not satisfied, but while you're in there, you need to be content to realize, 'This is where I am, so what do I do with where I am? "

Be where you are. Focus on what you have and where you are. You can't do something with where you're not. For example, say you don't have any money. You don't want to think, "Next month, I really won't have any money because I'd be 2 months behind on everything I owe." I don't want to be the person who keeps going further and further down pretending everything is okay.

Where you are is where you are. What actions can you take now to change the pattern? That is the magic. Think, "What I'm going to do is take it from here and move forward." Acknowledge where you are. Don't be too content. Be thankful that you are where you are so that you can then focus on where you want to be.

Clif: Years ago, I heard a phrase that stuck with me that perhaps not completely but adequately expresses what you are saying. The phrase was "inspirational dissatisfaction." Be content but uncomfortable enough to aspire to become more. I'm content in that I'm

IF YOU CAN'T CALM THE WATERS, LEARN TO RIDE THE WAVES

Clifton Anthony McKnight

aware of my blessings, but I'm inspired to know that my blessings give me the capability to do more for myself and others. **What else would you like to say?**

Elliott: Enjoy this day, remembering that every day is a gift. ✧

Elliott's "theme song" seems to be "Focus on what you have and be thankful." It has a great ring to it. Try humming a few bars and see where it takes you.

Years ago, Elliott shared the following quote with me, "Refuse to let circumstances alter your thinking and you will see circumstances grow into the image of your thought." I am not sure where or from whom he heard it, but it has been with me ever since. Consider the Serenity Prayer, "Lord, give me the strength to change the things I can and accept the things I can't and the wisdom to know the difference."

"One man's feast"...

It is all in how we think. Two people in the same place at the same time can have completely different experiences of an event. Some people love rollercoasters, while others wouldn't even consider riding one. The saying "One man's feast is another man's poison" pays tribute to the fact that people often have a varied experience the same events. What if you could influence 80% or even 30% more of what you experience in your life? Wouldn't you want to move the experiences toward

IF YOU CAN'T CALM THE WATERS, LEARN TO RIDE THE WAVES

Clifton Anthony McKnight

that which motivates and inspires? By making a conscious decision to look for the value, you invoke the process.

Not Just Why; Why Not?

Earlier, I discussed some thoughts written by Anthony Robbins, one of the world's foremost success coaches and students of personal development. In essence, he said, "We can influence the quality of our lives by the quality of the questions we ask ourselves." When you ask yourself, "Why can't I ever do anything right" or "How come I always get the short end of the stick?" We are in a very real sense, sending our psyche out to track down answers to support the questions and the premise they imply.

The questions we ask ourselves are not evaluated for accuracy. Rather, they are like facts for which we seek data to confirm. Much like the selected memory in the "qs Wheel or Will of fortune," we embrace only that which is consistent with the question.

The task, then, is to re-arrange our questions; our "self-talk" to a more positive and powerful syntax... Instead of "Why can't I ever do anything right," ask yourself something like "How can I consistently be more effective?" Rather than "How come I always get the short end of the stick?," ask, "In what ways can I create the most value from my efforts?" Try the audio series **Personal Power** and his book, Awaken the Giant Within. Visit tonyrobbins.com for his latest resources and events.

How to Succeed in Turbulent Times

IF YOU CAN'T CALM THE WATERS, LEARN TO RIDE THE WAVES
Clifton Anthony McKnight

STAR

Sayings

"We become what we think about." – Earl Nightingale

"Refuse to let circumstances alter your thinking, and you will see circumstances grow into the image of your thought."

"We can influence the quality of our lives by the quality of the questions we ask ourselves."
- Paraphrase Anthony Robbins

Thoughts

Stay connected. Look to others' success as inspiration and validation that success is yours as well.

Actions

1. Go back and review the "Will-o-Fortune." Write about or talk to someone else about two occasions; one when your expectations paved the way for a positive outcome and one when your expectations paved the way for a negative outcome. How can you use these experiences to assist you in the future?

2. Pick up the audio series **Personal Power** by Anthony Robbins and listen as you walk, commute or conduct some activity not requiring your full attention.

IF YOU CAN'T CALM THE WATERS, LEARN TO RIDE THE WAVES
Clifton Anthony McKnight

3. Assess a situation from another person's vantage point. Base your perspective from the other person's life experiences and priorities and close associations. Then, pretend you are the other person trying to understand your perspective. This can help in improving understanding, negotiation, and harmonious living.

4. At your earliest opportunity, assign yourself some "ME TIME" and go somewhere that renews you. Be still in body and mind. If you fall asleep, you probably needed a nap anyway.

Resources

- www.theleadershipacademy.org,
- George Jefferson

- NOW, Discover Your Strengths
- Donald O. Clifton and Marcus Buckingham

- Awaken the Sleeping Giant Within
– Anthony Robbins

- Youtube.com - Anthony Robbins

Chapter Four

Spirit, Mind, Body, Spirit

"One individual, even partially enlightened about a thing, can make a world of difference." - Clif McKnight

We are in a sea of connectedness. We live in and ride the spiritual waves of Life and Love. If we can see this, then we can drink deeply from this ocean and be refreshed.

If we persistently pollute this reality with worthless materials, ugly thoughts and negativity, we poison ourselves and our surroundings. We become blind to our potential, blessings and gifts. Hope within us is shaded from the life-giving light of Love and choked away by the sludge of doubt, fear, jealousy, arrogance and anger.

What we see on a physical level is first observed on a spiritual and mental level. I use the term "spiritual," in this instance, to represent the thoughts floating through our mind that are attracted to the pre-existing thoughts existing there. More accurately, I am speaking of *how* we are in our *Be-ing*. That part of us which observes connects

IF YOU CAN'T CALM THE WATERS, LEARN TO RIDE THE WAVES
Clifton Anthony McKnight

with the part that thinks, feels, and interprets. Our choices or decisions are based on these thoughts, feelings and interpretations. Revisit the *Will of Fortune*, and see if you can apply it to something significant in your life's desires.

As we grow in our recognition of our connection, we grow in our capacity to be a positive influence. Take education, for instance. Dr. Mary McCloud Bethune started a training school in 1904 for Negro girls that grew to become Bethune-Cookman University. It is rumored and written that she began with just $1.50 in her pocket (that's One dollar and fifty cents!) Dr. Mary Bethune was the only one of sixteen siblings to be born free of slavery. Her parents had purchased their freedom by the time she was born but they were still financially tied to the plantation of their former slave master.

From such meager beginnings, Dr. Bethune pursued a vision to provide education for Black people in the South who might otherwise not have been educated. She purchased a four-room cottage near Daytona Beach, FL. Soon after, she opened the Daytona Normal and Industrial Institute for Girls with only five students. Within two years, her student population increased to 250.

You may not have heard of Dr. Mary McCloud Bethune or Bethune-Cookman University but this historically Black institution has educated literally tens of thousands of students from around the globe over the years. That is indeed a great legacy.

How to Succeed in Turbulent Times

IF YOU CAN'T CALM THE WATERS, LEARN TO RIDE THE WAVES
Clifton Anthony McKnight

You may not have heard the name Wendy Kopp either, but it is likely that you have heard of TEACH FOR AMERICA, an organization that recruits the country's best and brightest college graduates--many from Ivy League institutions, to teach in the country's most distressed urban public education systems.

Wendy outlined the concept of Teach for America in her thesis while attending Princeton University. According to the John Kennedy Foundation, more than 12,000 exceptional individuals have joined Teach for America, committing to teach for two years in low-income rural and urban communities. Imagine how many students have been positively affected by one woman's vision.

One individual, even partially enlightened about a particular thing, can make a world of difference. Enlightenment often leads to the kind of passion, assuredness and steadfastness that inspires persistent action and awareness. Assuredness leads to desire and determination. Desire and determination leads to self-discipline. When coupled with faith, these ingredients can inspire the spirit to persist through turmoil and to re-dress distress.

Remembering the Success Wave

"Success breeds success." "It takes money to make money. " "Birds of a feather flock together." "Things come in threes." "Nothing succeeds like success." Sayings can go on and on but these have a common

IF YOU CAN'T CALM THE WATERS, LEARN TO RIDE THE WAVES
Clifton Anthony McKnight

thread. "Like attracts like" and "Keep that ball rolling." Once we accept that things tend to *head in the direction that they are going,* we can tap into the power of the universe to take us where we want to go.

There are three options that come to mind. 1] Determine how to harmonize with and benefit from the direction of the winds. 2] Determine precisely where you want to go and employ tacking to get there. Or 3] Let the elements and surroundings sink the ship. I will illustrate each of the first two. I suspect that life has offered enough insight into the third option but I will offer a quick example for that as well.

1] *Determine how to harmonize with and benefit from the direction of the winds.* An example of harmonizing with the direction of the winds is when someone notices a hot trend and joins it. Imagine that you were able to acquire wholesale rights to purchase large quantities of cell phones from a solid service provider. You acquired them at the point that mobile telephones were priced low enough for purchase by the average American population.

If you positioned yourself at the beginning of that trend to sell competitively priced mobile phones by observing others in the industry or by exploring transferrable strategies from other industries, you had the opportunity to earn a great deal of money.

2] *Determine precisely where you wish to go and employ tacking to get there.* Merriam Webster's Dictionary defines tacking in the following manner:

IF YOU CAN'T CALM THE WATERS, LEARN TO RIDE THE WAVES

Clifton Anthony McKnight

1 a: to tack a sailing ship
   b: *of a ship*: to change to an opposite tack by turning the bow to the wind
   c: to follow a course against the wind by a series of tacks
2 a: to follow a zigzag course
   b: to modify one's policy or attitude abruptly.

Tacking is a process of getting where we want to go by approaching from a different direction or a particular angle which allows us to work with the driving force that would, if approached directly, push against us. It would be like getting off the highway during rush hour and proceeding via a little known short cut.

Another example of tacking may be illustrated via the stock market. A stock plunges in a downward spiral. Instead of buying or selling the overpriced stock, one might *short* or *put* the stocks (to sell or buy based on an anticipated drop price and collect the difference.) To blindly buy high priced stocks that are falling or to sell your high price stocks after they have fallen is representative of # 3 below.

3] *Let the elements and surroundings sink the ship.* Follow the masses. When things keep going and going in the same direction, follow the herd and you risk catching the trend at its end, thus being left holding the proverbial bag. I've done it and it worked... against me. I was in the middle of refinancing some property because I had over-leveraged myself and the banks would no longer lend. Some might say they would not lend as freely. For me, they ceased lending. Now you got it, horror of horrors, my wife could say, "I told you so." If only that could

<u>IF YOU CAN'T CALM THE WATERS, LEARN TO RIDE THE WAVES</u>

Clifton Anthony McKnight

have been the worst of it [chuckle]. Continuous education, insight, teamwork, practice, being mentored and understanding your risk tolerance all contribute to effectively using 1 and 2.

What We Abuse or Do Not Use We Stand To Lose; So Choose...

I have been a poster boy for both sides of this conversation. When we eat well, move our bodies, stretch ourselves, think positively, feel appreciative, we tend to be healthier and happier. When we are persistently inactive, eat a poor selection of low fiber, high refined sugar, dead foods and crowd our minds with worry and disappointment, we set ourselves up for poor health. I have done both and I will tell you, overcoming the inertia to initiate a different direction requires a deliberate shift. From what I can see, this is true the majority of the time. Check into it for yourself and consider your next step.

As *you* consider your life, please look to every experience to provide something useful and conduct yourself accordingly. Sometimes, we make choices that counter our well-being and we do so consciously. You might smoke that cigarette or I might eat that second slice of cake. Perhaps the immediate pay-off is greater in the moment than the not so vividly perceived delayed benefit. Perhaps we are battle worn and fatigued. What is done is done. Consciously, you can decide to make the very most of your circumstance, to glean the lesson and

IF YOU CAN'T CALM THE WATERS, LEARN TO RIDE THE WAVES
Clifton Anthony McKnight

the opportunity within the errant decision or the *failed outcome* and choose a new possibility.

The Perspiration Wave – Worry, Fear, Hurt, and Pain – and Victory

I won't spend a lot of time on this subject. Most of us spend too much time on it already. Worry and fear tend to extend negativity beyond its normal lifespan. We worry about past or present things. They have happened or we see that they can happen at some point in the future but we let it affect us negatively in the *now*.

Of course, there is space for healthy concern. The proper amount of concern encourages you to create contingencies and can inspire one to minimize risk by educating herself. This is not only reasonable, it is appropriate and desirable. To not be concerned at all is to be unprepared.

Still, when we care so much about a person, a thing, or an outcome, it seems quite natural to spill into the realm of over concern or worry. The more we worry, the worse we feel and the more out of control we feel. Specific resources will be discussed in the next chapter to help you feel great about yourself amidst the chaos.

Below are a couple of things for your consideration that you may find useful. First, inform yourself. The possibility of moving towards certainty and away from doubt can be increased by simply gathering more information about your goal or task. Second, share the reward and share the risk. When the risk is shared, the

IF YOU CAN'T CALM THE WATERS, LEARN TO RIDE THE WAVES

Clifton Anthony McKnight

burden is often spread out as well. Also more resources become available as more insight is gleaned from each individual who participates.

Hey, when you get knocked to your knees, make the most of it. You are in perfect position to pray, to gain introspect, to regain your composure and perspective and thus, to take action and claim victory. Yes, it is natural to be fearful sometimes. If you find yourself fearful, just limit the dose and begin to focus on desired results. I have heard *that faith and fear cannot occupy the same space*. Focus on possibility and your fears will begin to dissipate.

The Perspiration Wave - Exercise, Practice the Real Deal

Focused effort is clearly the key to maximizing *Natural Talent*. Spectators, those standing on the sidelines taking no explicit, concerted actions towards their goals, have a tendency to point out as overnight successes, those who have been working towards *their* dreams for years and years. These overnight successes are deemed as lucky or simply as having connections allowing the onlooker to remain comfortable with their own inaction. Do not be fooled. <u>Persistent effort</u> and <u>intensity</u> of <u>thought/feeling and effort</u> are what **create**.

Our mind, our body and our spirit all share in this. The more we *exercise* them, the stronger they become. This principal is universal.

A master key of living begins when we involve ourselves so intensely about a thing that we *forget* or lose sight of ourselves. We *become one* with that which we are

IF YOU CAN'T CALM THE WATERS, LEARN TO RIDE THE WAVES

Clifton Anthony McKnight

involved. Interestingly, people who find themselves moving selflessly through life seem to experience greater self fulfillment. They are so engrossed in the mission that during struggle, they just maintain a sense of direction and determination. They are energized and stabilized by a cause greater than themselves.

Persistent effort generally requires cultivation before it becomes a habit. Getting clear about one's direction and priorities occurs when one taps into divine synchronicity, the Intelligence that creates possibility and underlies purpose. "Self-engineered" direction is, to my mind, a reflection of God's plan through you and for you.

How are we to actualize all that is in us if we do not tend to our vessel? I refer specifically to our physical health and well being but it is absolutely interconnected. It would benefit us greatly if we move our bodies and breathe deeply the goodness of life and love. The energy required to exist happily and effectively is magnified by good health.

There are many examples of those who have done well, making a difference to all whom they've encountered, who are not the picture of health and perfection. Use those examples for inspiration and to empower yourself to contribute now even as you continue to move towards healthier living. Look for representations of good physical, mental, emotional and spiritual health and literally keep those images in mind. Keep them present. Stack the deck in favor of feeling good. Think healthy thoughts. Take healthy actions. Reflect, take action and rejuvenate.

How to Succeed in Turbulent Times

IF YOU CAN'T CALM THE WATERS, LEARN TO RIDE THE WAVES

Clifton Anthony McKnight

Western and Eastern-educated medical practitioner Deepak Chopra points out that we are renewed cells, living in what appears to be the same body. Much like the literal sea, the waters that flow through the ocean are different, existing in one area at one moment and in a different space in another. Add to that fact that the environment also evolves and we can readily accept the thought that time provides a canvas for change. In that same way, we are different representations of ourselves from one period of time or another. Why do we look the same? Is it *cell memory* alone – or are we behaving in a way that perpetuates a particular cycle of cause and effect?

If we acknowledge that we have a new body every day and a *new day* every day, perhaps we can influence ourselves to occasionally acquire renewed energy and a renewed perspective. Excellence is attained when talent meets interest and sustained effort over time.

Michael Jordan was arguably the best basketball player of his time, yet he was far from the go-to guy on the baseball field. Why? He worked at basketball harder and longer and it was his gift. I don't know if he played organized baseball beyond high school prior to joining the minor leagues. Practice and preparation most certainly have a role in an individual's success. Change your thinking and you can change your life. Michael Jordan's skills on the basketball court were sharpened by years of drive, intensity and an ability to center himself when it counted most.

How to Succeed in Turbulent Times

IF YOU CAN'T CALM THE WATERS, LEARN TO RIDE THE WAVES
Clifton Anthony McKnight

The thought occurs that many other people worked hard and had passion and did not fair nearly as well. What is that all about? My response is to dedicate yourself first to getting clear about your gifts, your strengths and your purpose. Then whatever you endeavor to do will prosper. Be still and really reflect to the core that is pure unlimited possibility and begin there.

"Being" with Your "Self" (Mind, Body, Spirit)

It should be abundantly clear by now that the most important and influential living and breathing person in your life capable of making your dreams into a reality is none other than *little ole you!* Give yourself audience with divine possibility. Immerse yourself regularly into the inner sanctum of your mind and create a physical space-- a sanctuary for yourself as well. If you don't have them both, take the time to create them now.

Establish your ideal space to withdraw, regroup and rekindle. I have become so much more conscious of the surroundings I create for myself since focusing on this concept. Perhaps you will too. Give yourself the space to bring together body, mind and spirit.

Some element(s) of this concept may be very natural for you and perhaps different aspects are more natural for others. Can you appreciate how you might serve one another if you team up to combine your strengths? This is both the root and the fruit of it all. We cease activity long enough to connect with spirit and purpose. Our desires are expressed from the root of spirit

IF YOU CAN'T CALM THE WATERS, LEARN TO RIDE THE WAVES
Clifton Anthony McKnight

and manifest into the fruit of the physical. Persistent thought and energized activity move the inspired vision into reality. You may ask, "Can I really create that which is borne in your spirit?" To paraphrase Steven Covey's sentiment, you have a 'response –ability' to do so. Responsibility needn't be limited to obligation. Expand your notion of it to reflect capability and the ability to respond to your purpose.

Ruth Norris is one of the most spiritual person's that I know. She is loving, thoughtful, and in every positive way, she is giving. I have been privileged that she is my Godmother. Ruth is a devoted Christian and has always been willing to take in those in need. Godmother Ruth has truly weathered her share of tragedy. Over the years, she has lost family and friends. Her response to a recent tragedy in her life may shed light on hardships you may have endured in your life.

Interview – Ruth Norris

> *Clifton:* Again, this is an opportunity that you are providing the world; to get some insight into some of life's challenges and how you have navigated those challenges.
>
> *Ruth:* Well, because it is the Christmas season, my mind and heart really does go back and reflects upon a particular situation in my life that happened a year ago. It was the death of my son, Kendal. It was a pretty dramatic time, and even now when I reflect on it, I do have moments of sorrow but then I also have joy and

IF YOU CAN'T CALM THE WATERS, LEARN TO RIDE THE WAVES
Clifton Anthony McKnight

peace. Those are the things that God gave me at the time of his death.

Just to kind of reflect on what took place, he passed on July 8th, but I would say maybe about a week or two weeks prior to that, and I'm not sure which happened first, but I'll tell you these two things that I think warned me about what was coming. God does prepare us; you know that He does. If we take our time and think about it or reflect after a tragedy happens, we can see that He was right there with us, knowing what was coming forth and preparing us.

I was out for a morning walk and this young guy was coming down the street-- a very tall guy. It looked like the top of his shirt was ripped and his chest was bare. He was barefoot, walking not in a steady way, kind of wobbling, and appeared to me to be out of it (not aware of his surroundings). As I passed him, my heart kind of went out to him. I put him in prayer and asked God to take care of him because the first thing that I thought about was that he was on drugs or something. And of course, I reflected that upon my own son.

After asking God to help him and keep him, I turned around and looked at him, and he was still walking with no awareness of his surroundings. I don't want to put it on the Holy Spirit, but something inside of me said to call the police, and I did call the police. And I called with the feeling that I wanted him to get help, not for the police to handcuff him and take him away.

How to Succeed in Turbulent Times

IF YOU CAN'T CALM THE WATERS, LEARN TO RIDE THE WAVES

Clifton Anthony McKnight

When I called the police, I described the situation to him and I said, "I'm calling for you to give this young man help because he needs help." I told him where he was and hung up. I said a few prayers for the man and went on about my business. Then a day or so later, I received a gift of an album from a lady and on the album was a particular song called "Mercy Said No." It was playing in my car while on my way to see my oldest son, Owen.

By the time I got to Owen's job, I was in tears, I mean complete tears. The gist of the song was that this young person had been going through a lot in life, and it was just beating her to death. Finally, "Mercy Said No," told the devil he could not have her. That was the gist of the song. Mercy took over and came to know who the Lord was. The whole idea was that God or Jesus was looking out for her.

The devil was kicking the person up, down and around and God's mercy said, "No, no more." I then reflected on myself and all the things I had been going through and what I went through up to that moment, and how God had said those words "No more" and had mercy on me. I cried and cried and cried. Then I went on, got Owen and told him about it and played the song one more time.

Well, I can say that no more than a week or so later, I got up on a Sunday morning, came downstairs and I decided to sweep the front porch, of all things. When I came in the bathroom door on the first floor, the door

How to Succeed in Turbulent Times

IF YOU CAN'T CALM THE WATERS, LEARN TO RIDE THE WAVES
Clifton Anthony McKnight

was shut. I heard this gurgling sound. I knocked on the door and I said, "Kendal?" And he didn't answer. So I went in the kitchen and I heard the gurgling sound again, When I came back and knocked again, I said, "Kendal open the door…open the door." And he didn't open it.

That went on for a time. I called my brother Teddy downstairs to help me get the door open, and we had this key to open the door, but it wouldn't open. Kendal was up against the door so we couldn't push it open either. Then I called Owen and then called 911. Owen got there before the ambulance because he lives closer. He tried to open the door and was able to get it opened a little bit, just enough so that I could see the bottom part of Kendal's body lying on the floor with the needle and syringe. That's when I knew he had been in there taking drugs.

The police came and Owen rushed me upstairs. I am grateful to this day he did that because I can still see Kendal on the floor because we had gone outside on the porch and I got up on the chair and was able to look through the bathroom window. I couldn't open it because we had a lock on it so you couldn't open it through the outside.

And I could see him bent over; he had been on the toilet and had fallen forward, and it was his shoulder that was against the door which was why there was so much weight against the door. When I saw his back, that's when I thought to myself, "I don't believe that he

How to Succeed in Turbulent Times

IF YOU CAN'T CALM THE WATERS, LEARN TO RIDE THE WAVES
Clifton Anthony McKnight

is alive." By that time, Owen had come and tried to get the door open and the paramedics came and everybody sent me upstairs.

As I reflect on it, as I was praying, I was saying, "Just one more time, Father, just one more time." But they were more words than a prayer because I believe now, that he was gone and there was no need to pray any more. And then Owen came upstairs and told me he was gone. I believed that God would receive him in Heaven and that he would not go to hell.

It wasn't his death that I was upset about; it was that I did not want him to be in hell.
Kendal didn't know God and Jesus. He had given his life over to Jesus and had gone to class but wasn't able to hold onto it. I remember he stood at my door one night, and he banged his chest and said, "I've got to focus, I've got to focus, I've got to focus." He was trying but he just could not get past those drugs. When he died, I prayed "God please, please," and I cried unto the Lord…oh God, did I cry, to "please receive my son, and do not let him go to hell."

I tell you Clifton, when I finished praying, the peace came over me. It was God's answer to me that He had received my son. I was so at peace with all of this that when people came to pay their respect, there were no tears. I had no tears to shed. I was joyful and the people who came and offered prayer were good, kind and generous. Even at the funeral, I had no tears to

How to Succeed in Turbulent Times

IF YOU CAN'T CALM THE WATERS, LEARN TO RIDE THE WAVES
Clifton Anthony McKnight

shed. It was because God had given me His ultimate peace, and I knew it in my heart.

Clif: What have you learned? What else would you like to say?

Ruth: Other than to believe and trust more in God, I would say one of the most important things that I have gained from all of this is that there is nothing like the peace of God. Peace from God. I pray for a lot of things in life. I have a lot of emotion, as do most people. There are things that we don't understand, things we're dealing with, so we ask God to help us, teach us, and show us.

But I tell you, my best times are when I have the peace of God, when I experience that peace of God that is way down inside. That, as the scripture says, it is way beyond understanding. It is just there. I can feel it and almost touch it because it's so real and so deep. And I know when I come out of it, somehow I have allowed something to distract me. I go back again, and I pray for that peace.

I just felt it the other day when reflecting on Kendal. I could still feel the peace even though there was that sorrow from the fact that he wasn't here anymore. It still was the kind of peace a knowing that he's ok. And with all the sadness and unhappiness that he experienced in his mortal life, I know he is not experiencing that pain anymore, and I believe that with all my heart.

How to Succeed in Turbulent Times

IF YOU CAN'T CALM THE WATERS, LEARN TO RIDE THE WAVES
Clifton Anthony McKnight

You know, you hear a lot of people saying things about how they think they're going to see folks when we die. I have no idea what God is planning-all this eternal life that we will experience. It's alright with me whatever way He decides to do. But I believe somewhere, somehow, Kendal's spirit and my spirit will be together again. Whether or not we recognize each other as son and mother, there will be a joining of spirits, and I do look forward to that day.

By experiencing a loved one's death, if I were to say anything to anybody, it would be to immediately ask for God's peace and let it flow over you. Everything will go well and you'll be fine. I don't know if any other gift that we could receive from God than His peace because peace to me speaks that I have faith in Him and the utmost trust in Him.

When I can experience the peace that I'm talking about, I don't worry about anything, and if something happens during the course of the day, I know God is there with me, and things will work out. You know that scripture about you not worrying because you can't change anything? Well, that peace will keep you from worrying. I am telling you, there is nothing like the peace that God will give to us, to fill our souls, minds, spirits, and our hearts. There is nothing like His peace.

To me, God's peace is saying how much He loves me. He showers His love down on me, and because His love is so strong, I can feel this peace that I have. So if I were to say anything to anyone about the loss of a loved one,

IF YOU CAN'T CALM THE WATERS, LEARN TO RIDE THE WAVES
Clifton Anthony McKnight

just ask for God's peace. And when I pray for someone in times like that, it's always for His peace.

Clif: I thank you for that because sometimes, when I am informed or become aware of someone in my circle that has lost a loved one, I have been at a loss as to what I can do. That is a good answer right there. I can pray for God's peace to rest upon them.

Ruth: Yes. And I received a card when Kendal died, and I passed that card onto different people. In it, it basically told me that I can grieve in whatever way I want to grieve; if I want to cry, cry; if I want to scream, scream; if I want to do whatever, to go right ahead and do that. And so, I say that to people--just grieve the way that you feel, but always remember that God is there. Don't let God out of the picture. Keep Him in your picture. And then I pray for the peace of God for them.

But you know when people say, "Don't cry. He's in a better place now," I try not to go there because they know a lot of the *spiritual things* that you're going to say. I just say you go right ahead; if you want to scream, you go right ahead; if you even want to be angry with God, you go right ahead, but always believe that God loves you, don't ever let go of His hand.

When I have peace with God, my spirit is completely united with His and there is nothing in between. There is no fretting, there is no "Lord help me with this," there is no whatever; it is a surrender to Him. He is the almighty and I am His child and because I am His child,

IF YOU CAN'T CALM THE WATERS, LEARN TO RIDE THE WAVES

Clifton Anthony McKnight

He loves me so much that He just sends that love down in droves of peace.

When I don't have peace, I know it, and I'm not happy. I have experienced His peace well enough to know when I don't have it. And then I ask for His peace, and that just simply means that my faith and trust is back in Him completely.

Clif: So, if I ask you how you are doing, would you say that you're at peace or you are well or you're still heavy in the question? I've heard all of those things.

Ruth: When people say to me, "Hi, how are you doing?" I just say that, "I am just well; thank you, I am just truly well." That "well" says everything for me; it doesn't just mean I'm physically well, it means that I am being taken care of by God. If you can recognize…I mean *truly* recognize…the smallest thing that God does for you, if you see that you know that was God, then you do have peace.

A lot of times, I think that we look at the big things that God does for us, and we think "God is good.." Also with the bigger, more tangible things, we say "God is good." But I tell you when you can look at the tiny things that God does for you--and I know it probably sounds silly, like times when I had gone somewhere and didn't know the direction, and all of a sudden there was either the street that I was looking for or the street that I was familiar with enough to where I want to go. , *That ain't nobody but God.* If you are late going somewhere and the parking lot is full and lo and

IF YOU CAN'T CALM THE WATERS, LEARN TO RIDE THE WAVES
Clifton Anthony McKnight

behold, there is a parking space almost at the door, that is God at work.

I fell yesterday-- I fall all the time and each time I get up, and brush myself off, I might have some skin abrasions, but I ain't got no broken bones. That's God. That is Him taking care of me. I stumble all the time, but I don't fall down *all the time*. That is the Lord Jesus Christ taking care of me.

Just little, tiny, itty bitty things let you know that He is in your life. I mean He is all over my life. When it comes to finances, somehow or another, I tell you, Clifton, I have been down to 60 bucks to last me the rest of the month. Then I went to a filing cabinet and stuck down in the side of the drawer was 200 bucks. And that is just one time; I could tell you 3, 4, 5, 6 times He has done something similar. That is no one but God. He is in everything we do. There is nothing that we do when God is not there.

And you can recognize it within your relationship with Him. You find the peace, you're not fighting; you're not scrambling; you're not in woe all the time. You find that when you go to Him and praise him, you're at peace. When you're not always asking for things for yourself, you know you are in peace.

If you don't have trust and faith, then you never had peace and you need to go back and try and get it by putting more trust and faith in Him and asking for His

How to Succeed in Turbulent Times

IF YOU CAN'T CALM THE WATERS, LEARN TO RIDE THE WAVES
Clifton Anthony McKnight

peace. That is what I got from Kendal's death; I can tell you there was nothing like the peace.

I would imagine that some people are wondering what in the world is wrong with this child. She has just lost a son and she acts like she hasn't lost a son at all. The Lord kept me at peace. I was at peace because I knew Kendal was with God.
Clif: Well, that's a mouth full; it is indeed… Godmother Ruth, thank you.
Ruth: Let me just say a prayer unto the Father so that it will touch somebody's heart. ✧

Ruth Norris remains an inspiration to those who have the good fortune to cross her path. It is my sincere hope that you may draw the insight and inspiration from this interview. Stay tuned. There is more to come.

How to Succeed in Turbulent Times

IF YOU CAN'T CALM THE WATERS, LEARN TO RIDE THE WAVES
Clifton Anthony McKnight

STAR

Sayings

"The last thing to do when you fall down... Get Up. "
— Clifton McKnight

"A setback is a set up for a come back. " — Willie Jolley

"Success breeds success."

"Faith and fear cannot occupy the same space."

"Birds of a feather flock together."
"Things come in threes."

"Nothing succeeds like success..."

"Like attracts like."

Thoughts

"One individual, even partially enlightened about a thing, can make a world of difference. " — Clif McKnight

This came from an email sent to me:

*"Look back and thank God.
Look forward and trust God.
Look around and serve God.
Look within and find God!"*

How to Succeed in Turbulent Times

IF YOU CAN'T CALM THE WATERS, LEARN TO RIDE THE WAVES

Clifton Anthony McKnight

Actions

1. Identify three things within you that deserve expression. Bring them together to form one vision.
2. Prioritize (or confirm) your commitment to see it through. Give energy to your vision by imagining and asserting that its destiny will manifest within you.
3. Decide what you are willing to do to bring your desires into expression.
4. Schedule your desired date of achievement
5. Begin doing it now.
6. Build a team with diverse talents who will commit to mutually support your best interests.
7. Re-visit goals frequently and evaluate your progress. Give yourself feedback and get external feedback as well.
8. Make adjustments and watch them unfold. Celebrate the milestones along the way.
9. Create/visit your inner sanctum today. Refresh yourself.

Resources

Ageless Body and Timeless Mind -Deepak Chopra

The Game of Life and How to Play It - Florence Scovel Shinn

How to Succeed in Turbulent Times

IF YOU CAN'T CALM THE WATERS, LEARN TO RIDE THE WAVES
Clifton Anthony McKnight

Think and Grow Rich - Napoleon Hill

Think and Grow Rich, A Black Choice – Napoleon Hill and Dennis Kimbro

Yahoo.com Search – Wendy Kopp - AmeriCorp

http://www.pbs.org/wgbh/amex/eleanor/peopleevents/pande05.html
- Mary McCloud Bethune

How to Succeed in Turbulent Times

Chapter Five

How to Feel Great About Life (Even in Turbulent Times)

"One ship sails east and another sails west with the self-same winds that blow. Tis the set of the sail and not the gale which determines the way they go" – Ella Wheeler Wilcox

News flash! If you are alive, you have problems. Okay, maybe that's not news to you but it is noteworthy. Consider this- problems can sometimes be a good thing.

When I am in the midst of struggle, if I am not mindful, a "woe is me" or "Why me?" attitude might take root in my mind. The truth is that struggle is as much a part of life as comfort, and it contributes to growth. How we relate to struggle defines a great deal of what we experience and how it helps us or stunts our growth.

There are three resources I'd like to highlight:
1] Prayer and meditation (spirituality);
2] People (relationships and support); and
3] Perspective (detachment and surrender.)

IF YOU CAN'T CALM THE WATERS, LEARN TO RIDE THE WAVES

Clifton Anthony McKnight

These are very broad and very deep resources. When the waters are terribly turbulent, you may elect to use all three.

Sometimes in our lives, events occur that totally upset our equilibrium. Our whole constructed reality can be shaken. A significant loss or a major setback can leave us whirling, struggling just to maintain sanity. During such times as these, it is more than helpful; it is often essential to call on PRAYER POWER.

Prayer Power- Take Inventory - Count Your Blessings... Regularly

So much happens when we pray. I'll point out my experience and consider what could occur for you. I usually settle myself down by ceasing all activity for the moment. I just stop. This allows me to center myself. This act is very valuable and the prayer process has only just begun.

I have been taught to begin with acknowledgement and gratitude. The effect of projecting that there is a source and a force capable of handling any situation which provides me with an audience and sustenance calms the emotions. The gratitude creates a whole new vibration in my spirit. At this point, I have opened myself up to receive more blessings.

Most often, I am thinking even more clearly and in essence, attracting positive results. I have a progressive attitude regarding my circumstances and have possibly been endowed with a perspective where the value of the

IF YOU CAN'T CALM THE WATERS, LEARN TO RIDE THE WAVES
Clifton Anthony McKnight

moment or at minimum, the perception of a better day may be imagined. A verse in the Old Testament, Isaiah 65:24 of the Bible comes to mind, "Before they call, I will answer." Before I realize I have a need, the solution is on its way. Imagine how you would feel when that realization visits your consciousness. Cool your heels for a few moments, and revitalize yourself with a prayer.

The more you pray, the more you connect. The more you connect, the greater your capacity to forgive, to live and let live, while constantly striving to help make the world better. You aren't just setting yourself up to receive a blessing; you are positioning yourself to BE A BLESSING.

One of the most under-rated principles on the road to happiness and success is the principle of *Counting One's Blessings*. By this I mean taking the time to really appreciate all the good things you have experienced and all that is good RIGHT NOW. Counting your blessings opens you up to the wealth of the universe. It also paves the way for further gratification. When you appreciate what you have, you automatically create the capacity and magnetism to receive more.

If you find it difficult to notice your blessings, it's is a very good indicator that you have been so blessed for so long, that you now take your blessings for granted. You may unconsciously feel a sense of entitlement which minimizes your awareness of your gifts.

If you are reading this book, you have eyes to see <u>and</u> you can read. If you are listening to a recording, you can hear. You have the space to read (or hear) this. This

IF YOU CAN'T CALM THE WATERS, LEARN TO RIDE THE WAVES
Clifton Anthony McKnight

is just the beginning. You have to look where you are right now and be thankful for your situation. Even if you are reading this from the jailhouse, I am sure there are many who don't eat as much as you. I think you get the idea.

By focusing on your blessings, you engender a spirit of gratitude. An attitude of gratitude lifts the spirit and provides one with a welcoming demeanor. In your social and business transactions, which personality types attract you? Would you gravitate toward someone who is critical, pessimistic, narrow-minded and selfish or someone who is genuine in spirit, warm, welcoming, and optimistic? Indeed, there is a place for all elements, and you may benefit by clearly deciding which characteristics you care to embody. We tend to gravitate to what we prefer. Focus on the positive.

Consider the alternative. Focus on negativity and negativity persists. We have bad experiences once when we hold on to them. They continue to haunt us and control our experience of life as we revisit them. I received an email called "The Sack" that I'd like to share with you to illustrate this point.

Unload Your "Sack of Potatoes"

A teacher once told each of her students to bring a clear plastic bag and a sack of potatoes to school. For every person they refused to forgive in their life's experience, they chose a potato, wrote on it the name and

IF YOU CAN'T CALM THE WATERS, LEARN TO RIDE THE WAVES

Clifton Anthony McKnight

date, and put it in the plastic bag. Some of their bags were quite heavy.

The students were then told to carry this bag with them everywhere for one week, putting it beside their bed at night, on the car seat when driving, next to their desk at work. The hassle of lugging this sack around with them made it clear the amount of weight they were spiritually carrying. They also had to pay attention to it all the time so they would not leave it in embarrassing places. Naturally, the condition of the potatoes deteriorated and emitted a nasty smell and slime. This, in turn, made the potatoes unpleasant to be around.

It didn't take long for each of the students to figure out that getting rid of the potatoes was much more important than carrying them around. This is a great metaphor for the price we pay for keeping our pain and heavy negativity. Too often, we think of forgiveness as a gift to the other person. Forgiveness clearly is important for all of us.

IF YOU CAN'T CALM THE WATERS, LEARN TO RIDE THE WAVES

Clifton Anthony McKnight

FEAR   GRUDGE   PAIN   *By Chelsea McKnight*

I don't know the source of this story, and I do not remember the first person who made it available to me, therefore, I am ever "paying it forward." Let go of hurt feelings, resentments, and regrets. Replace such thoughts with forgiveness, understanding, and even love. This may take some practice. It will absolutely be worth it.

Create a Commercial

"Huh? Create a commercial!?! You gotta be kidding." Look, I understand that to some people, these suggestions may seem too *radical*. Ask yourself though, "Am I willing to try a few things outside of my normal behavior in order to create above normal results for my life?" There is no risk here. There is only possibility and opportunity.

How to Succeed in Turbulent Times

IF YOU CAN'T CALM THE WATERS, LEARN TO RIDE THE WAVES

Clifton Anthony McKnight

Think about your good qualities and your strengths as you see them. Now list all of the positive qualities you know about yourself and add those that others have said about you in the past. Do not dismiss or edit anything. You might even contact a few close friends and *ask them* to pretend that you have just commissioned them to develop an ad campaign to promote the best in you. Try it.

Next, imagine that you represent a high- powered wall street advertising firm and you have been given the task of marketing a product called you to the world. What kind of commercial would you develop? What vehicles would you use to promote the brand of *"you?"*

As you write the script, bear in mind that just as it is done for most high powered products, a *"brand"* should be identified that defines the character or essence of *you*. Your core features and benefits should be communicated. Don't just deal with who you have been, address who you are and who you intend to be.

The best commercials evoke an emotional response. They make us laugh or they make us reflect. What will you come up with here? Who can assist you in developing your commercial? Most marketing executives work with a team. Enlist the support of co-workers, friends, and loved ones, and reciprocate if invited.

Consider creating a poster or a professional or visual document of some sort that you can review often. Note the pleasant surprises and the reinforced qualities that you most appreciate. Sit for a moment, and consider how fortunate you are that you had the kind of

IF YOU CAN'T CALM THE WATERS, LEARN TO RIDE THE WAVES
Clifton Anthony McKnight

associations that appreciate you enough to participate in this project.

People - Ride with the Tide - Associate with People Who Believe In You

Have you heard the colloquialism, "You can do bad by yourself"? How about, "Birds of a feather flock together." Sometimes, your self-confidence is not as strong as you would like it to be. This is the very time that others will come along to confirm that you can't do it or can't have it. If you let them, they will break you down. You can reverse this self-defeating tendency by surrounding yourself with strong minded people, people who are headed somewhere and who recognize that you are, too!

Family, friends, associates, even characters you meet through books [wink] can be a resource when you are open to the positive support. It is all within your circle and within your reach.

IF YOU CAN'T CALM THE WATERS, LEARN TO RIDE THE WAVES

Clifton Anthony McKnight

Perspective

I came across a quote appropriate to this discussion that you might find useful. I was reading <u>ON TRACK ON FIRE ON PURPOSE</u> by Barbara S. Talley, friend, author, speaker, entrepreneur, publisher, and mother of six (6), and she referenced the words of Norman Vincent Peale which said, "Life's blows cannot break a person whose spirit is warmed at the fire of enthusiasm." Taking the time to establish a task or goal that you intensely desire to accomplish can be a major contributor to your happiness.

Open your being to possibility. Tune your frequency toward joyfulness. Recognize that peace, possibility, and perfection are in you. You can take time away from the world's woes and access joy at will.

While flipping the channels one Sunday, I came across a Christian pastor named Joel Osteen. His sermon (I think it was #368) harmonizes with what follows. Essentially, the point is this, you and I "are." We are each special and unique, and what is before us to do is <u>for us to do</u>. When we come across someone who is doing great things, we can celebrate their accomplishments and recognize them as examples of the potential we have to be our highest and best selves.

We needn't compare ourselves to another in a negative way. We are who we are, and they are who they are. The true value in observing others' success is in being happy for them and having reaffirmed that we can

How to Succeed in Turbulent Times

IF YOU CAN'T CALM THE WATERS, LEARN TO RIDE THE WAVES

Clifton Anthony McKnight

reach our own personal zeniths. Like musical artist Bobby McFerrin said, "Don't Worry. Be happy."

You probably know that when we are happy, we smile. Are you aware also that when you smile, you become happy? This is far truer than most can imagine. What happens when you smile at someone around you? The late billionaire, philanthropist Sir John Templeton wrote, "Living life with a smile is like throwing yeast into a bowl of flour, adding warm water and waiting for the flour to rise, it multiplies many times over." So, one really straight forward strategy for feeling better is to simply smile more. Do not dismiss this because of its sublime simplicity. You owe it to yourself just to experiment with this very simple, free action. Don't wait for "Candid Camera," just go ahead and smile.

WE, you and I, make the world a better place. The influence we have is staggering. We could say, on the other hand, that we have very little control. We don't control accidents, we cannot control the weather and these are things that can change our lives in the blink of an eye. This can also be freeing if you think about it.

To the extent that this is so, why spend so much time worrying if we can't do anything about it? Still, it tends to happen. I worry, too, more often than I'd like to admit. Yet, even as I write this, I know in my heart of hearts that I can fall back into a position of strength. Too often, I will have stressed a bit before waking up to the wastefulness of my psychic energy.

IF YOU CAN'T CALM THE WATERS, LEARN TO RIDE THE WAVES
Clifton Anthony McKnight

Redress Distress for Success

Have you ever noticed how some people seem to always be happy? Or have you ever seen someone who is in a worse situation than you appear to be feeling just fine? If, when you think about it, you have noticed either of these scenarios, *celebrate!* This is an indication that you have not been entirely blinded by your own circumstances; you aren't so consumed with your problems that you have suffocated your potential for growth and happiness. You can take a break from your issues and focus on someone else's. You feel capable, and you give your spirit connection space to transmit the answer.

There are levels and varieties of strategies and techniques for calming the waves within. I came across a list of strategies for coping with stress so extensive that one might gloss over it because of its size. It is a far better approach to look at a few strategies and let them sink in a bit. To be sure the list is still immensely incomplete. Add what works for you. It just gives us more to look forward to.

As I look into my life, there are a few things that work for me that might not be on the list, such as having a snack or scheduling a meeting with a friend in an environment that revitalizes me, such as the lobby of a very nice hotel that combines nature with extravagance. Better yet, have lunch. Of course, this can be extended to incorporate renting a room and taking the FAM on a mini vacation within 50 miles of home.

How to Succeed in Turbulent Times

IF YOU CAN'T CALM THE WATERS, LEARN TO RIDE THE WAVES

Clifton Anthony McKnight

Here are a few strategies, 101 to be exact, adapted from the Mental Health Association in Greater San Antonio by the Rockville Maryland Mental Health Association. A colleague passed a copy to me, and you can use it to de-stress and feel great about yourself:

101 Ways to Cope With Stress

1. Meditate
2. Relax under the shade of a tree
3. Listen to relaxing music
4. Read junk mail
5. Visit an art gallery
6. "Say no" more often
7. Set priorities in your life
8. Rent classic films
9. Use time wisely
10. Simplify meal times
11. Buy yourself a present
12. Anticipate your needs
13. Take a walk at sunset
14. Look at problems as challenges
15. Take a drive in the country
16. Color in a children's coloring book
17. Be yourself
18. Give a rival a compliment
19. Look for the silver lining
20. Teach a kid to fly a kite
21. Walk in the rain
22. Avoid negative people
23. Schedule some play time every day
24. Take a bubble bath
25. Believe in you
26. Turn off the news
27. Laugh

How to Succeed in Turbulent Times

IF YOU CAN'T CALM THE WATERS, LEARN TO RIDE THE WAVES

Clifton Anthony McKnight

28. Visualize yourself winning
29. Dance a jig
30. Set goals for yourself
31. Have a picnic in the park
32. Hug a friend
33. Gaze at the stars
34. Breathe slowly
35. Read a poem
36. Listen to a symphony
37. Sing in the shower
38. Take a child to the zoo
39. Leave everything a little better than you found it
40. Plant flowers every spring
41. Stop blaming others
42. Count your blessings
43. Eat a chocolate ice cream cone with a child
44. Read the comics
45. Watch a ballet
46. Pick wildflowers
47. See a "G" rated movie
48. Watch Bugs Bunny cartoons
49. Take stock of your achievements
50. Find support from others
51. Travel somewhere new
52. Be cheerful and optimistic
53. Do something in support of others
54. Travel somewhere new
55. Avoid bringing your work home
56. Strive for excellence not perfection
57. Read your horoscope with a friend
58. Look at pictures from your past years
59. Hum a jingle
60. Maintain your weight
61. Plant a tree on your birthday
62. Feed the birds
63. Practice grace under pressure
64. Stand up and stretch

How to Succeed in Turbulent Times

IF YOU CAN'T CALM THE WATERS, LEARN TO RIDE THE WAVES

Clifton Anthony McKnight

65. Take a nap on the couch
66. Doodle
67. Tell a joke
68. Make a milkshake
69. Learn to meet your own needs
70. Become a better listener
71. Take a trip to the beach
72. Daydream
73. Volunteer your time
74. Take charge of change
75. Make a paper airplane
76. Exercise
77. Sing a song out loud
78. Go to bed early
79. Read a romance novel
80. Play patty cake with a toddler
81. Write an old friend
82. Take a different route to work
83. Take a cool shower
84. Put on a T-shirt and kick back
85. Call a long distance friend
86. Wear a funky tie or hat to work
87. Go to a little league game and cheer
88. Eat a meal by candlelight
89. Recognize the importance of unconditional love
90. Chew gum
91. Bake homemade cookies and eat them fresh out of the oven
92. Keep a journal
93. Read a children's book
94. Visit a different church
95. Remember you have options
96. Have a support network of people
97. Quit trying to "change" other people
98. Try a new menu item
99. Freely praise other people
100. Read this again

How to Succeed in Turbulent Times

<u>IF YOU CAN'T CALM THE WATERS, LEARN TO RIDE THE WAVES</u>

Clifton Anthony McKnight

101. P.S. Relax, take each day a time…you have the rest of your life to live.

Mental Health Association
1000 Twinbrook Parkway
Rockville, MD 20851
301-424-0656
Fax: 301-738-1030
E-mail: <u>info@mhamc.org</u>
<u>www.mhamc.org</u>
Adapted from Mental Health Association
Of San Diego

As aforementioned, the only problem with such a great list is that we tend to skim over it and think, "That's nice." Give yourself the space to explore these suggestions deeply and experiment with the strategies that resonate with you.

People and Prayer for When the Tsunami Comes

Now, think about the people you love helping. Why is it that when you do things for them it actually makes your day? One reason might be that they greatly appreciate all you do, and they show it. Sometimes, they simply express their gratitude and sometimes, they joyfully rush forward to return the favor. The same holds true on a deeper, personal level. Love others, genuinely, and you have a greater *experience* of love. There is an adage that resonates with this, "Love is like perfume.

How to Succeed in Turbulent Times

IF YOU CAN'T CALM THE WATERS, LEARN TO RIDE THE WAVES
Clifton Anthony McKnight

When you put it on someone, you can't help put get some on yourself."

Family can be a wonderful source of support. Even in the most troubled of waters, perhaps particularly in the most troubled of waters, friends and family can represent a reservoir of mutual support.

Few have had to endure turbulence like Sunilda Zabala and her family.

Interview - Sunilda Zabala

Suni and I spoke at length. After discussing the questions, we scheduled another occasion to conduct the interview.

> *Suni:* The most challenging moment in my life was my mother's death. My mother and father were walking somewhere. My Father was in front; my mother was just a few steps behind. My father crossed the street and looked back and did not see her. He hadn't heard anything and did not see anything. We notified the police. I was constantly in prayer for her well being. We were to discover that she was already gone.
>
> We learned later that my mother was hit by a truck and dragged a mile and a half down the road. The driver wasn't even aware that he had hit her. They found her on Gude Dr. God had answered my prayers by touching someone's heart to stop oncoming cars in the middle of the road to prevent them from further mauling her body.

IF YOU CAN'T CALM THE WATERS, LEARN TO RIDE THE WAVES
Clifton Anthony McKnight

I have always been a person of a lot of faith… This was and is hard… I try not to think about it. There are many questions that cannot be answered.

We were very close. I visited her every weekend. I am grateful that my Mom visited Columbia Thanksgiving 2005. It was her first time to return to Columbia in 10 years. My mother felt really happy that she had the opportunity to go for 5 months, and I was happy for her.

Mother got a lot done. She took care of some affairs. She also had somehow managed to spend genuine quality time with each of us most recently including those who were sometimes hard to reach. She usually went to the beach with her husband and, this time in July, she went with me and again in August she went with my [other] sister.

These days, holidays are toughest. On the positive side is how we are as a family. We are so much closer now. Many gifts were left by Mom. Memories and her humility are two gifts. Also, Mom was a very humble person. Perhaps the greatest gift she left us is forgiveness. Forgiveness is good for everyone.

I work and stay busy with the kids. Sometimes I felt like I could end up in a mental institution. The week before Sept 26, 2006 was 2 yrs.

IF YOU CAN'T CALM THE WATERS, LEARN TO RIDE THE WAVES
Clifton Anthony McKnight

What have I learned? I don't look at life in the same way. I am more conscious about living. Every moment counts. I think God prepares you for that.

Clif: What suggestion do you have for others?

Suni: Visit your loved ones REGULARLY. It would have been worse if I hadn't done that with my mother.

Clif: What else would you like to say?

Suni: Be together. When 9/11 happened, people began to realize that they need to be together more. We were always together, and now we are still closer. Even the ones who tended to be out there are closer.

9/26 was my 9/11. People, the police, friends, family, co-workers really offered there support in so many ways. Sometimes, we tend to see the police based on negative things. You know, they want to give you a ticket or something. The police were so helpful and sensitive. How [tactfully] they found and confirmed that it was my mother. How they communicated, cared, and even fed [us] while [we] were wondering what happened. I have 13 brothers and 3 sisters, and those who have activities and relationships help to keep you going. ✧

People and prayer can be all the difference. Everything we do can have more light and color when we embrace our spiritual source and one another. Give yourself pause, and embrace your grace.

How to Succeed in Turbulent Times

IF YOU CAN'T CALM THE WATERS, LEARN TO RIDE THE WAVES

Clifton Anthony McKnight

STAR

Sayings

"Love is like perfume. When you put it on someone, you can't help but get some on yourself." - Unknown

"Smile when you say that."

"Before they call, I will answer." - Isaiah 65:24, the Bible

Thoughts

"One ship sails east and another sails west with the self-same winds that blow. Tis the set of the sail and not the gale which determines the way they go" – Ella Wheeler Wilcox

"Life's blows cannot break a person whose spirit is warmed at the fire of enthusiasm." - Norman Vincent Peale

You probably know that when we are happy, we smile. Are you aware, also, that when you smile, you become happy?

"Living life with a smile is like throwing yeast into a bowl of flour, adding warm water, and waiting for the flour to rise; it multiplies many times over." – Sir John Templeton

"Forgiveness is good for everyone." -Suni Zabala

Actions

How to Succeed in Turbulent Times

IF YOU CAN'T CALM THE WATERS, LEARN TO RIDE THE WAVES
Clifton Anthony McKnight

1. What sacks are you carrying? Look it over. Smell it? Leave it behind. Go ahead. You can do it. How do you feel now? Write about it, or talk with someone about it.
2. Think about a time where something occurred that challenges the notion of "coincidence." Revisit the experience at length. Keep your eye open for more of these small miracles.
3. Many people will not have done the commercial. Did you?
4. Take 10 minutes (with pen in hand even) and tell yourself who you choose to be. Write, reflect, write some more.
5. Another approach is to engage in discussion with people who you know have your best interest at heart. Share with them some of what you have been reading and what it is you have been thinking as a result.
6. Grant others the privilege of your ear. Listen to their responses and observations. You will have done them a great service, and you might learn a bit more about yourself.
7. Write down their observations without edit, and go back to look for the nuggets that you can use to propel you forward.
8. Visit that *YouTube* thing again on the internet. Check out Norman Vincent Peale, Bobby McFerrin – "Don't Worry Be Happy," Joel Osteen
9. If you don't want to do this right now, go back to the Will of Fortune and reread it. You deserve the time. You are worth it.

How to Succeed in Turbulent Times

IF YOU CAN'T CALM THE WATERS, LEARN TO RIDE THE WAVES

Clifton Anthony McKnight

Resources

ON TRACK ON FIRE ON PURPOSE – Barbara S. Talley

http://thepoetspeaks.com

http://www.barbaratalley.wordpress.com
http://www.mhamc.org

http://www.mhasd.org

How to Succeed in Turbulent Times

Chapter Six

Perspective - Get a Panoramic View of the Ocean

"It's all in how you look at it."

When things are at their worst, we often are at our best. You probably have heard the aphorism that "Struggle builds character." Far more often than not, this is true. Still, I know I am not the only one who sometimes feels weary of building character. I want to say, "Enough with the character building already!" Fortunately, we are equipped with a survival mechanism. There is little else to do but to act, pray, and endure. Giving up is the least attractive option.

   I was granted time away from work in order to focus on this book and to revitalize. The gift of being afforded time on a meaningful project cannot be measured. It has been the kind of blessing that offers longstanding benefits to me, to my family, to my college community and prayerfully to you. Life's challenges did not halt just because I was on a mission to complete this

IF YOU CAN'T CALM THE WATERS, LEARN TO RIDE THE WAVES
Clifton Anthony McKnight

work. You know the drill, financial turbulence, intense health and family issues, the not so small stuff, still competed for my attention. I could and sometimes did add to the distress by thinking, "Woe is me."

From the sidelines, I'll bet you can readily see the ridiculousness of such thinking. Once I really thought about it, I realized that though I had issues to address, I also had the gift of additional time to address them. I was granted space to write, to reflect, and to carry out the various tasks necessary to significantly move the book project toward fruition. These issues and projects would have still persisted without my having the leave from work! Health, family illness, and other challenges are as much a part of the process of living as anything else.

It is critical that we gain and maintain perspective as often as we can. In maintaining perspective, we give attention to the "Important" as well as the "Urgent" as author Stephen Covey would say. Important speaks to critical long term issues while urgent might speak to loud, attention getting *not necessarily* important issues. With perspective comes focus. Focus invokes intensity and intensity gets things done.

So, we look at the bigger picture of what is important to us in the long term. We move from there to determine the specific day to day activities that we need to accomplish what we want. Then we act on those plans to get and do what is most important to us.

Stephen Pierce, motivational speaker and internet marketing expert, contends that while most think that consistency has to be developed we already have

IF YOU CAN'T CALM THE WATERS, LEARN TO RIDE THE WAVES

Clifton Anthony McKnight

consistency. We are consistently doing what keeps us from what we want or we are consistently doing what brings us to what we want. We simply need to change our direction.

While for some this may be grossly oversimplified, it offers a peek into the reality that all that we need already exists in us. We seem to be forever in the quest of getting what we need before we can have what we want. We are stressed out because we need more time, more money, more love, more expertise, more stuff, more, more, more. Once we come to recognize that we can make better use of what we ALREADY HAVE, *"More"* will beat a path to us.

A few decades ago there was a popular song in my circle entitled "Express Yourself." In recent years, I have heard a portion of it in one of the many *fine* commercials on the air. There was a phrase in the chorus that you may remember, "Some people have everything that other people don't, but everything don't mean a thing if it ain't the thing you want. Express Yourself."

Some of the heartache we experience can be minimized *simply* by putting things in perspective. Putting things in perspective via the panoramic view also positions us to see the greater need; those needs which stem well beyond our personal circumstances. Ending poverty hunger, homelessness, crime war, disease, or responding to natural disasters are a few problems that deserve our attention.

When we consider the greater need and determine to contribute to the solution, something happens within

IF YOU CAN'T CALM THE WATERS, LEARN TO RIDE THE WAVES

Clifton Anthony McKnight

us. We experience a sense of new found strength, a sense of empowerment that can readily spill over and add capacity to solving our personal needs. We also experience an expanded sense of community.

Often, insight into the many problems of the world can bring us more in touch with our blessings as well. The more in touch with our blessings we are, the more we tend to be relaxed. When we are relaxed, our resourcefulness has space to explode into creative problem-solving. Further, our spirit is energized to carry out these previously untapped strategies.

With perspective, we can persist through moments of disappointment and setbacks. When we recognize the dips and don'ts as temporary road signs to success achievement, we are less likely to falter. So, when things are darkest, recognize that you are closest to the dawn.

Persist and Succeed

Years in preparation, focus, distraction and deviation
Disappointment and jubilation
Lead to the here and now with great syncopation,
Such a script life has wrought in every nation.
All that is required is our active participation.

Life comes at you fast.
Sometimes "it's a gas" sometimes you're aghast.
Draw upon resources present and past
Persist and tribulations you will outlast

How to Succeed in Turbulent Times

IF YOU CAN'T CALM THE WATERS, LEARN TO RIDE THE WAVES

Clifton Anthony McKnight

> Prosperity will surely be amassed.
> Persevere, faith overcomes fear
> Seeded actions make opportunity appear.
> *Clifton A. McKnight*

Over the years, my father has become somewhat of a hermit. He often refused to go out or be around people. You see, Dad had lost most of his eyesight and is hard of hearing. Not having learned appropriate coping mechanisms and suffering from some of the additional challenges of aging, it became essential to his well being that he live with someone. Presently, he lives with my brother Steve a great percentage of the time. He was spending about 90% of his time in his room. One night when I was with him, he said that he thought he may want to venture beyond the door of his bedroom sometime and start to learn about what is around him. What he said resonated with me on a deeper level. He said, "That door is not the end, it is the beginning."

It strikes me on other levels that the same could be said about the door between the known and the unknown. This is also true about birth. A baby is born by being forced out of one environment or experience, the womb, to a new unknown reality. The same could well be true about death. Death is not the end; it is an introduction to a new reality, a new beginning.

Nearly everything in between gives birth to the next thing... The door closes for one job and on the other side lies a better job or the inspiration to start your own business. A relationship ends, and the knowledge and

IF YOU CAN'T CALM THE WATERS, LEARN TO RIDE THE WAVES
Clifton Anthony McKnight

experience prepares you for a better one. We are more because of our experiences when we remain open and in positive anticipation. As the years go by and the winter years bring their chills to your bones, remember the saying, *"If it's winter, spring can't be far behind."*

Remember Your True Nature

From where I sit, it is clear that we are all related. We are connected so completely that it seems almost ludicrous to think otherwise. Still, to the extent that we want for ourselves and those in our more immediate circles more so, consider how the "Golden Rule" has been expressed by religions and philosophers throughout history.

The Bahai faith makes reference to five religions with assertions to treat one another well. They read:

> *"Hurt not others in ways that you yourself would find hurtful. – Budhism*
>
> *What is hateful to you, do not to your fellow man. That is the Law; all the rest is commentary. –Judaism*
>
> *Do unto others as you would have them do unto you. – Christianity*
> *No one of you is a believer until he desires for his brother which he desires for himself. – Islam*
>
> *Blessed is he who prefereth his brother before himself.*
> *- Bahai Faith*

How to Succeed in Turbulent Times

IF YOU CAN'T CALM THE WATERS, LEARN TO RIDE THE WAVES
Clifton Anthony McKnight

I came across websites that compiled even more representations of the "Golden Rule." Take a moment next time you are in front of a computer and Google the "golden rule," "religions" and you may find as many as 21 different religions represented, all encouraging us to be mindful of one another's needs.

Mayhap we get the message! To be of service to others is to serve one's self. If you really want to get jiggy with it, consider <u>The Platinum Rule</u>, a concept pinned in a written work of the same name by authors Tony Alessandra & Scott Zimmerman. The "Platinum Rule ®" takes the "Golden Rule" a step further by suggesting that *"You do unto others as they would have you do unto them."* Think about it, and you may appreciate the wisdom in the sentiment.

Understand the Value of the Rain - Transmutation and Gleaning Good From All things

I have been working diligently over the years to build two companies while working full time as a Professor/Counselor at Montgomery College in Rockville, Maryland. The challenge has been more harrowing than I care to admit. Further exacerbating the situation were life events which tended to distract if not derail my efforts.

I dedicated a great deal of energy researching, identifying, viewing, and assessing properties 50 to 100 miles away regularly and hundreds of miles

IF YOU CAN'T CALM THE WATERS, LEARN TO RIDE THE WAVES

Clifton Anthony McKnight

intermittently. I invested a great deal of time learning about real estate as I went about trying to inspire and inform people at work and around the country through my other company. At the same time, I sought and accepted public speaking and training opportunities, prepared presentations for delivery, and conducted presentations on leadership and personal development.

For a time, it was energizing even invigorating setting and reaching new goals touching lives in a variety of ways. I am not sure when it started. Off and on, I seemed to be getting tired. Eventually, I started feeling tired all the time. Some would suggest that my plate "runneth over." Indeed, my plate was quite full, but so was my cup. I strived to be true to my capacity, and I endeavored to balance my approach utilizing systems and human resources as feasible. Operating with a mind set of limited resources dictated that I carry and wear many hats myself.

Between 2004 and 2005, my health issues rose to impair my overall effectiveness. I "passed out" as a result, of all things, from stifling laughter. I had become "tickled" because my wife was having a serious talk with one of our daughters and, based on the look on my daughter's face, it was clear that her sentiment may not have been sinking in. I did not want to complicate things by laughing.

Over the past 30 or 40 years, there had been 5 or 6 occasions where I would laugh until I felt light headed and might even lose my equilibrium. Still, I felt good, and it would pass without incident. However, on this

IF YOU CAN'T CALM THE WATERS, LEARN TO RIDE THE WAVES

Clifton Anthony McKnight

occasion, I lost consciousness at the top of the stairs resulting in my tumbling down the stairs. As I said, this occurred as a result of my attempt to stifle a laugh. We (my wife and I) decided to check it out in response to the second occasion and the shorter period in which the previous episode took place.

My doctor assessed my issue to have been a rare but typical (sounds like an oxymoron to me) effect of an "irritated vagus nerve." It was rare in that laughter isn't a highly reputed cause and typical in that the result is "harmless," brief, unconsciousness. I tried to shake off my concern and carry on. It is more likely that the incidences and the declaration of a potential condition that might predispose me to "passing out" affected my overall efficiency.

In August of 2006, I passed out again trying to talk as a laugh was about to erupt. This time I was behind the wheel. The result of my state was a severe accident whereby I totaled the vehicle that I was driving with my wife, youngest daughter, and older daughter's friend in tow. Fate (I say God and his Angels) would have it that NO ONE WAS SEVERELY INJURED physically and no other vehicle was involved. My wife had some scratches from the broken glass, and my daughter had a bump on her head.

For months after the event, I found myself struggling at first and just managing at best. I was surprised at my feebleness when so many have recovered far more effectively from far worse. Still, my health was in question as I had "passed out" – again, and behind the

IF YOU CAN'T CALM THE WATERS, LEARN TO RIDE THE WAVES

Clifton Anthony McKnight

wheel at that. My human frailty was exposed. I became slightly disoriented for an extended period due to worry and quiet desperation, the opposite of what I desired.

My physician postulated that the cause was once again, a vaso-vagal response. The vagus nerve is a very long nerve which goes from brain to abdomen. According to Wikipedia,"Vaso-vagal syncope is caused by the triggering of a paradoxical reflex, which causes a **fall in blood pressure** and loss of consciousness." http://en.wikipedia.org/wiki/Vagus_nerve For quite a while, I was not confident about driving and had to be driven to most places. When I finally grew confident enough to drive for any length again, I found myself overly cautious and stressed. Driving lost its ease.

What was I to do? My primary means of transportation in business is by automobile, AND I commute to work! In realizing how much my life and the lives of my family depended on my having the ability to drive, I was a bit pre-occupied from my other duties, including getting the tax returns out on time. I have established safeguards for safe driving. As for my returns, well, we have our extensions done on time [smile].

I revisited death's door again about a year later. Like the rest of us, I was dealing with life, you know, family issues, work issues, disasters, and global issues, when I developed an infection which spilled into my blood stream resulting in a state of Sepsis. **Sepsis** is a condition in which your body is fighting a severe infection.

How to Succeed in Turbulent Times

IF YOU CAN'T CALM THE WATERS, LEARN TO RIDE THE WAVES
Clifton Anthony McKnight

If you become "septic," you will likely be in a state of **low blood pressure** termed "shock." This condition can develop either as a result of your body's own defense system or from toxic substances made by an infecting agent (such as a bacteria, virus, or fungus). http://www.emedicinehealth.com/sepsis_blood_infection/article_em.htm. I was told that had I gone 24 more hours untreated that I might not be here today. I completed many tests. I am a large body and an "over fifty" adult, but I exercised far more than the average mature adult. I was confused about being weak enough to fall prey to sepsis.

I read an article that included the passage below:

> "People whose immune systems (the body's defense against microbes) are not functioning well because of an illness (such as cancer or AIDS) or because of medical treatments (such as chemotherapy for cancer) that weaken the immune system are more prone to develop sepsis. It is important to remember that even healthy people can suffer from sepsis. It typically strikes people who already have an underlying illness compromising their resistance."

In a related section, I found, "Men with an enlarged prostate: Prostatitis or obstruction of the urethra by an enlarged prostate can lead to incomplete bladder emptying, thus increasing the risk of infection. This is most common in older men." Well, I am but a young pup in my fifties, so I clearly am not an older man [smile]. Still, it happened, and it can happen to anyone. For more information, see the website,

How to Succeed in Turbulent Times

IF YOU CAN'T CALM THE WATERS, LEARN TO RIDE THE WAVES

Clifton Anthony McKnight

http://www.emedicinehealth.com/sepsis_blood_infection/article_em.htm.

While the suspected underlying culprit was prostatitis, the possibility of reduced immune function due to stress has been presented as a distinct contributing factor. Further, it was determined that the chronic fatigue (which I seldom acknowledge) that I still occasionally experience is partially due to Severe Sleep Apnea. I am currently under treatment. The statement that "It [sepsis] typically strikes people who already have an underlying illness compromising their resistance" suggests that I have a few things to battle. The article also iterated that "The elderly population, especially those with other medical illnesses such as diabetes, may be at increased risk as well." I am maturing and not yet elderly, but as a result of all the tests to surmise my condition, my physician discovered that I am Hypoglycemic or "pre-diabetic."

So, where is the good in all of this? First, with this awareness perhaps I can head off becoming diabetic. Second, as a result of all the tests, I discovered that I was in the early stages of prostate cancer. What's so good about that? I was able to obtain treatment early and perhaps extend my life once more.

The real question is "Do I and do you get the point?" As I look to "find the good," I acknowledge up front and personally that it would have been far better to have taken steps to be healthier than to have gone through this. I have taken notice and begun making adjustments. I am moving forward on getting my

How to Succeed in Turbulent Times

IF YOU CAN'T CALM THE WATERS, LEARN TO RIDE THE WAVES

Clifton Anthony McKnight

"music" out to the world and counting my blessings far more regularly.

Alright, there may not literally be "good in all things" for us. Still, all things may be transmuted to "work for good." We can approach every experience as if there were a lesson we could gather from it thereby making us better. **We can uncover and we can create** something in spite of the worst situations and we can use the worst situations to strengthen us, to offer insight and wisdom or to appreciate another's plight.

Maureen Edwards, PhD – Interview

Maureen Edwards holds a doctorate in Health Education from the University of Maryland at College Park. Her areas of specialization are Stress Management and Gerontology. Dr. Edwards is also certified as a Master Health Education Specialist (MCHES). In addition, she has received advanced training by the Critical Incident Stress foundation as a post-traumatic stress debriefer and has been trained by the American Cancer Society to conduct smoking cessation workshops.

Currently Maureen serves as the coordinator of both the Health Education and the Aging Studies programs at Montgomery College Rockville campus. Whenever our paths crossed we shared a kind word or a warm hug.

Following a chance interaction, Maureen took the time to write this account for you.

How do we do this?

How to Succeed in Turbulent Times

IF YOU CAN'T CALM THE WATERS, LEARN TO RIDE THE WAVES

Clifton Anthony McKnight

I was sitting at my desk preparing for the new semester when I heard the voice of a friend in the hall. I went out to say, "Hi and Happy New Year." He asked me how I was and instead of the superficial, polite, "Fine, how are you?", because I know he really does care, I found myself telling him that my Uncle had just died.

Not only my Uncle, but my favorite Uncle, the one who bought you ice cream before dinner even though it would spoil your appetite, slipped you a couple of dollars when Mom wasn't looking, and somehow always managed to win you the big stuffed animal at the church carnival. In short, my Uncle Harry was a big kid.

What made his passing even more poignant was that he died in the same hospice, same room, same bed as my Mother, his oldest sister. When Mom was dying, I remember asking the hospice nurse, "How do you do this, look at the face of death everyday and keep coming back for more?" I'm sure she must have been asked that question hundreds of times, but she smiled and told me that every once in awhile when it starts to get to her, she does a few rotations in maternity to remind herself that "It isn't all about endings, there are beginnings as well."

A couple of days later, Mom died, and the hospice called and asked if the family wanted to come and see her to say a private goodbye. We arrived together, Dad, my older brother, and me, and we checked in at the nurse's station. The nurse that had so compassionately

IF YOU CAN'T CALM THE WATERS, LEARN TO RIDE THE WAVES
Clifton Anthony McKnight

cared for Mom offered her condolences, and I know she was sincere.

While Dad and my brother made arrangements for Mom, the nurse asked me if I was okay and at that moment, I was. She took my Dad's hand in her right, my brother's in her left, and I trailed behind. As we walked to Mom's room, I was struck by how these big strong men clung to this little woman like a lifeline.

During Uncle Harry's service, I found myself thinking how "topsy turvy" the world felt. Over the past few years, I had lost my mother, father and now Uncle Harry. I felt overwhelmed by loss and angry that death had taken yet another dear one.

As if sensing what I was feeling, my husband reached over and took my hand. Even in the midst of grief, I found myself feeling lucky that I didn't have to do this alone. I thought about my friend Jerry who has been like family to me for almost 30 years sitting behind me offering support and Nancy and Phil who had a warm hug and a hot meal waiting when we got home.

It was then that I realized I had answered my own question. How do we get through times and events like these? The answer is together. ✧

In life, there are those things that can mar us if we are not careful. I strongly recommend obtaining support and assistance when devastating or atrocious events occur. It is consistent with the "Will of Fortune" to use

How to Succeed in Turbulent Times

IF YOU CAN'T CALM THE WATERS, LEARN TO RIDE THE WAVES

Clifton Anthony McKnight

"all of our strength." A strong spiritual connection and introspection represent a primary source of comfort and strength which can be experienced and magnified through the "human angels" that walk the earth.

It makes good sense to seek spiritual, psychological, and emotional support in particularly turbulent times. Hey, it makes sense to regularly build these channels of support and to make "emotional deposits" as often as you can. Steven Covey talks about relationships being built with "emotional bank accounts." He suggests that, in relationships, we are always making deposits or withdrawals. It offers a vivid analogy doesn't it. Pick up a copy of THE SEVEN HABITS OF HIGHLY EFFECTIVE PEOPLE on CD or the book and watch the possibilities in your life expand.

Seek the *positive* lesson. That lesson which fosters whatever you and your world need. Napoleon Hill said, "Every adversity carries with it the seed to an equal or greater benefit."

We all have heard something to that effect before. "Trial and tribulation builds character." "Hardship and sacrifice make you stronger." And, sometimes, I want ... some rest; to feel good; to have my cake - and yes, to eat it, too!

William James once said, "Human Beings can alter their lives, by altering their attitudes of mind." People do not experience joyous living because good things always happen to them. They experience joyous living because, among other things, they choose their perspectives and

IF YOU CAN'T CALM THE WATERS, LEARN TO RIDE THE WAVES
Clifton Anthony McKnight

responses to what happens to them. Rough waters exist in all lives.

Okay, this is TOUGH. How does one stay positive, hopeful, productive, and focused when one's very survival is constantly at stake? And what about horrors of mass proportion or glaring events which depict mans' inhumanity to man? Pray, pray, pray...

Individuals like Nelson Mandela, Viktor Frankl, Martin Luther King Jr., Mary McCloud Bethune, and the many martyred civil rights leaders are magnificent models of dedication, altruism, and forgiveness. These great souls are only a few examples of what thousands have done who miraculously maintained their sanity and their resolve in the face of imprisonment and the constant threat of death. They have gone on to make MAJOR contributions to their community, their country, and to the world over.

Some of these individuals survived for years as actual political prisoners and/or prisoners of war. Others dedicated themselves to battle hatred, imprisonment, prejudice, and discrimination. Surely we can make it through life's twists and turns.

In reading a copy of Black Enterprise (BE) Magazine, (October, 2007), I learned of Ishmael Beah. The last page of this issue offered me insights from a young man who as a 12 year old was deep in the throes of a vicious civil war, all but devastating the peoples of Sierra Leone. How does one rebound from such horror and devastation at such a young age? Ishmael spoke of transforming the experience rather than attempting to

IF YOU CAN'T CALM THE WATERS, LEARN TO RIDE THE WAVES

Clifton Anthony McKnight

forget it. He suggests that since some of the pain runs so deep let the experience be instructional and perhaps guide us to be more appreciative of each breath we take. BE noted the role UNICEF played in rescuing and rehabilitating Mr. Beah and referred to his book, A LONG WAY GONE, MEMOIRS OF A BOY SOLDIER.

During my tenure as a professor and counselor at Montgomery College, I had the privilege of meeting and working with many valiant souls, co-workers and students who served as models for transmuting pain and tragedy into hope strength and possibility. These brave souls were additional sources of strength, wisdom, and support for me during some of my most trying times. Family and extended family and friends offer rich sustenance to fortify us during times of need.

Well, get ready. If times have been hard and you have gleaned the lesson, then prosperity is sure to follow. For sure, everything is not as we want it to be, but it is important to note that everything is unfolding perfectly when we are connected with the rhythm of the universe.

We can all agree that there are many things that occur in this world that the world can do without. There is no conflict in acknowledging this.

"Human induced suffering is not required. It certainly is not desired. Our gift is that we can use it to be inspired.

Inhumanity, suffering, and pain call for an inspired response of humanity, charity, and gain." – Clif McKnight

How to Succeed in Turbulent Times

IF YOU CAN'T CALM THE WATERS, LEARN TO RIDE THE WAVES
Clifton Anthony McKnight

"It ain't simple," but it is real. We can transmute negative to facilitate positive. We can be inspired to take action against it. Given the choice, I surely would prefer to go directly to the positive, but I cannot always determine that. I can only determine, in time, my response to it. Let me be quick to add that, often, it takes significant effort to do so.

Can't sleep at night? Use the time to work on a task or concern that has been bothering you. It just may be the very thing that is keeping you from sleeping. At the very least, you can feel good about completing or resolving something important instead of tossing and turning all night leaving yourself with the same issues in the morning.

Another option is to redirect your focus to you blessings and a prayer of gratitude until you fall asleep. This can actually result in a rather restful sleep, enabling you o approach the following day and your problems with a fresh new energy. You may be amazed at how effective a strategy this is. Like most other exercises, it will get easier with practice.

IF YOU CAN'T CALM THE WATERS, LEARN TO RIDE THE WAVES

Clifton Anthony McKnight

STAR

Sayings

"It's all in how you look at it."

"Human Beings can alter their lives, by altering their attitudes of mind." -William James

"If it's winter, spring can't be far behind."

Thoughts

Yes, you are dying... It may take eighty to one hundred years or so, but you'll get there. In the meantime, do yourself and the world a favor, live until you die.

"Happiness comes from spiritual wealth, not material wealth... Happiness comes from giving, not getting. If we try hard to bring happiness to others, we cannot stop it from coming to us also. To get joy, we must give it, and to keep joy, we must scatter it."
  - Sir John Marks Templeton

"The more you pray, the more you connect. The more you connect, the greater your capacity to forgive..."

*"Persevere, faith negates fear.
Seeded acts make opportunity appear."*

"Human induced suffering is not required. It certainly is not desired. Our gift is that we can use it to be inspired.

How to Succeed in Turbulent Times

IF YOU CAN'T CALM THE WATERS, LEARN TO RIDE THE WAVES
Clifton Anthony McKnight

Inhumanity, suffering, and pain call for an inspired response of humanity, charity, and gain." – Clif McKnight

"How do we get through times and events like these? The answer is, "Together." – Dr. Maureen Edwards

Actions

1. Try focusing on your blessings 3 days in a row. Write them down, think about them, and review your lists. Even tell a few people a few of your observations, insights, and appreciations, especially if it includes them.
2. Visit the library or do an online search for the names William James, Nelson Mandela, Martin Luther King Jr. Mary McCloud-Bethune, and Victor Frankl. Do this even if you are familiar with the names. Where does this take you?
3. Can't sleep at night? Redirect your focus to your blessings and a prayer of gratitude until you fall asleep.

Resources

The Seven Habits Of Highly Effective People – Dr. Stephen Covey Book
Discovering The Laws of Life – Sir John Marks Templeton

www.mhamc.org - Mental health Association of Montgomery County

IF YOU CAN'T CALM THE WATERS, LEARN TO RIDE THE WAVES
Clifton Anthony McKnight

Black Enterprise Magazine, October, 2007

http://www.azvictims.com/coping/default.asp - State of Arizona Crime Victim Services

http://harmonhouse.net/fdl/quotes.htm - Freedom digital Library, Quotes

http://www.professionalchaplains.org

http://en.wikipedia.org

A LONG WAY GONE, MEMOIRS OF A BOY SOLDIER - Ishmael Beah

How to Succeed in Turbulent Times

Chapter Seven

Self-direction - Where Are You Headed?

"Everything is on its way to somewhere." – <u>Phenomenon</u> – *MOVIE*

There are **many** who are willing to tell you where to go, but to reap your greatest benefit you must be true to yourself. Choose to identify and accept your life's purpose and be about that business. The choice to accept sheds light and intensifies a magnetism that orders and clarifies your steps.

View It from the Mountain-Top

The highest point you can find is usually the best vantage point for determining where you are headed. It is also useful to appreciate how you arrived at where you are. To understand your present state is to establish a reference point, the "YOU ARE HERE" marker, if you will. Reflect on this, and write down thoughts that come to you. It can be a very effective exercise to help you

IF YOU CAN'T CALM THE WATERS, LEARN TO RIDE THE WAVES
Clifton Anthony McKnight

clarify your direction and to notice your progress (or lack thereof). Look back and retrace the thought path that brought you here.

Then as you look around to interpret your surroundings, you can decide on the direction you are headed and the life you desire. You can begin to visualize the outcome you have in mind. A clear awareness of a starting point and end goal greatly facilitates one's sense of direction.

We can borrow processes from successful organizations to use in our personal lives. For example, successful organizations use vision statements and mission statements to establish their purpose and their process. Just as organizations use these tools to order their steps to keep them on course, you can establish your own vision and mission statements to assist you in staying on target. It might not start as clearly defined as you want, but it will become more clear as you venture forward.

The beauty is that a clear vision can get and keep you going, moving forward through meaningful life experiences. It connects the dots. It offers meaning to challenges and difficulties. It fosters persistence. Purpose or vision provides us with additional fortitude to deal with life.

Do you agree that YOU deserve to have a purpose or mission in life? If not,stop, reflect, and re-read. Purpose provides direction and stability. In tumultuous waters, it is very helpful to have something stabilizing on which to hold. What I love about this is that purpose can

IF YOU CAN'T CALM THE WATERS, LEARN TO RIDE THE WAVES
Clifton Anthony McKnight

seldom be superimposed. It can be inspired and, in a healthy environment, purpose is self-generated.

In <u>The 7th Habit of Highly Effective People</u>, Dr. Stephen Covey says our mission statement (purpose) represents a kind of compass that keeps us on track. In <u>The Eighth Habit,</u> Covey later wrote about "Finding your voice and helping others to find theirs." By "voice" I believe Mr. Covey means "Purpose" or even "passion." If reading this piques your interest, you may want to pick up a copy of <u>The Eighth Habit</u>. I found his work to offer a technological approach identifying and methodically following your passion.

Leaders of companies and countries take purpose seriously. It would serve you well also to take this to heart. You are the leader of a company called YOU. Establish for YOU and for the world your own identity, your own brand, if you will.

Lawrence Milan, Senior Vice President, Human Resources, ING Americas, and Tavis Smiley, political commentator and talk show host, both emphasize the importance of establishing your own personal brand. Leading business schools refer to it. You are the CEO who determines how YOU will interact and contribute to the world.

In Man's Search for Meaning, Viktor Frankl wrote: "Ultimately, man should not ask what the meaning of his life is, but rather must recognize that it is he who is asked. In a word, each man is questioned by life; and he can only answer to life by answering for

IF YOU CAN'T CALM THE WATERS, LEARN TO RIDE THE WAVES
Clifton Anthony McKnight

his own life; to life he can only respond by being 'responsible'."

You set the guiding principles for carrying out your purpose.

Obtain Your Map or Draw It

Most of the things we build in this life require a plan, a map, or a blueprint. "Times are hard. " Everywhere you turn, you can find doom and gloom if you look for it. Times are absolutely magical, as well. Never in the known history of this world have we come to have the resources we have today. Those of you born in the 70's and 80's or more would be served well to learn how it was for the average person technologically during that time and before. The word "incredible" comes to mind when I look at it. What we take for granted today was virtually science fiction to many who were teens or older in the 70's or before. How did we get here?

What will the next 20 years bring? It will likely mirror today's science fiction and more. Mapping out outrageous goals is a major step in the direction of outrageous attainment. Map out the life you want, design how you intend to get it. Expect results.

It is just what is done when someone wants to create a building. First, the building is designed and blueprints are drawn. If you decide to drive to a far away destination, what must you do first? You plan it out, get directions, or ask someone. You check your budget. You

IF YOU CAN'T CALM THE WATERS, LEARN TO RIDE THE WAVES
Clifton Anthony McKnight

"map it out." In the 21st century, you may chart it on your GPS.

Though plans may and often do change along the way, the likelihood of a satisfactory conclusion of the task, building, or vacation is far more likely when it is mapped out on paper or computer. Surely your life is no less important. Examine the past and present. Observe the trends of the day paying close attention to what successful people do to accomplish their goals and get started.

Learn the Lay of the Land ... and Sea (See)

Having a vision for yourself and a plan to attain your vision are the "active ingredients" to the recipe for successful travel through life. Still, it is important to pay close attention to detail and to be on constant look-out for the subtle things which can make all the difference. These are often conveyed as unwritten rules and cultural idiosyncrasies. Learn well your surroundings, your path, and your inner workings, and you may find yourself far more able to manage turbulence than others.

Nearly every endeavor has an art side and a science side. Learn the mechanics and BE the work. That is, make the pilgrimage an extension of who you are rather than something you do. Who do you think will be more successful, the person who strives to be the most valuable player or the one who resolves to be the difference that her teammates need to win? Get intimate with your path. Learn the nooks and crannies, the

IF YOU CAN'T CALM THE WATERS, LEARN TO RIDE THE WAVES

Clifton Anthony McKnight

potholes and mud holes. How? Think about it all the time. Practice, do. Ask, research, "Be." Study the geography of your task. Who is in it? Practice immersion... Immerse yourself.

Make it difficult to distinguish your self from your mission. See the vision as if it is already real – and it will be. Smell, taste, touch. Let your muscles react as if you were truly in it. This way of being creates an almost physical magnetic field attracting in the ethereal that which you have so vividly embraced.

Choose Your Vessel

I believe many of us over-ponder, delay and defer rather than choosing a path. Once the end desire is clear, the vessel, the vehicle, needs to be selected - AND ENGAGED. One can reach a destination by walking, driving, or flying. As a matter of course, all three modes of motion may indeed play a role.

When we have invested the time to psychically and emotionally connect ourselves, it can seem as if the vessel *selects us*. At minimum, one feels like the vessel resonates in a way that just *feels right*. Listen to your inner voice. Give credence to your intuition, and explore your hunches, even your small quiet ones. Your career or business idea or charitable passion or whatever it is will become evident.

Your "hunches" often occur early. I often say to myself, "God is whispering in your ear. Don't have Him get out the two by four to get your attention. You don't

IF YOU CAN'T CALM THE WATERS, LEARN TO RIDE THE WAVES
Clifton Anthony McKnight

have to run into the hornet's nest to understand that it is a bad idea. Remember, experience may be the best teacher, but other people's experience can save you a whole lot of heartache while you learn."

As you hone your intuition and research the history of things, you may discover that you can take the distress out of choosing your first vehicle by observing what your predecessors used that worked. People who have attained what you desire in times past and present are magnificent models to be explored. Remembering that most journeys involve a variety of modes of transportation should help you relax more and not fixate on choosing the "perfect" vessel.

Anything that moves you forward *is moving you forward*. You can tweak as you educate yourself. As the times change, your vehicle will likely change, or your use of it may change. Ride the wave; go with the flow.

Stocks, real estate, starting a business, buying an existing system or franchise are all possibilities. Partnering with people who offer talents, resources (financial and otherwise), and contacts complementary to yours represents one of many excellent strategies for making things happen. Resources are broad and varied. Communications regarding how to make "IT" happen are offered through multiple venues. Tap them all. Books (remember the library?), seminars, classes, mentors, magazines, and the internet are just a few resources within our reach.

How to Succeed in Turbulent Times

IF YOU CAN'T CALM THE WATERS, LEARN TO RIDE THE WAVES
Clifton Anthony McKnight

Test the Waters – Often

Feedback is of greatest value when objectively assessed and then presented with an appropriate response. Back up and look at the whole situation from a variety of angles and make the appropriate response. Who decides what response is appropriate? *You do*! Own your response and your ride will be your adventure.

Set Your Course

I heard Tom Peters of McKenzie Associates say once, "Ready! Shot! Aim!" While that may sound a bit reckless, I think it speaks to an issue which plagues many. Many people deliberate on what they should deliberate about before beginning to consider the possibilities regarding the varieties of directions and the potential obstacles and issues…. [chuckle and moan]. It is called the paralysis of analysis. This is why so many never get out of the starting blocks.

There comes a point when you have to trust yourself, to trust your instincts, and that point usually comes after you take action.

Set Your Sails (self-programming)

Enter old telephone directory commercial; two vintage Cadillacs collide and two Elvis impersonators get out. One says something like, "Hey, who do you think you are hitting my car!?" The other says, "Uh, Who do you think,

IF YOU CAN'T CALM THE WATERS, LEARN TO RIDE THE WAVES
Clifton Anthony McKnight

uh, I think I am?" As a character of the late Richard Pryor used to say, "That, is the eternal question." Who we desire to be and what we desire to accomplish is a choice that we had better make for ourselves because there are many people out there who would do it for us, on their terms.

Others have to make sense of their world so they define every thing including us based on their construct. They may even attempt to define us, TO US, on their terms. That's right: if we do not take expressed, personal responsibility, rest assured, there are a world of others out there who will delegate what *they want* of us and define us through their jaded glasses.

Reserve your right to choose. It is a human inheritance that deserves embrace in a deliberate way. We are responsible, "response able" when we consciously choose.

I'd rather be wrong because of my own decision than to dismiss myself and subjugate to another's mandate. It is one thing to see the merit in someone else's perspective, but it is folly to totally discount your inner thoughts and assessments. At the end of the day, you choose.

Cast Your Net (Taking Action)

Plan it, schedule it and do it! Reflect, adjust, and take more action. There are many resources that offer time or life management tools. The bottom line is ACT NOW for that is what is. "Yesterday is history.

IF YOU CAN'T CALM THE WATERS, LEARN TO RIDE THE WAVES

Clifton Anthony McKnight

Tomorrow is a mystery. Today is a gift. That's why they call it the present." – <u>Kung Fu Panda</u>. Of course, similar quotes come from esteemed philosophers and orators, but isn't it great that wisdom is available in children's films? On a more serious note, if you research Mother Teresa, you may find a very similar quote encouraging us to act now. The only time that one can act is in the present. If you find procrastination is an obstacle for you, set the book down for 10 minutes and start something that you have been putting off that is important to you.

Have you returned after 10 minutes? Did you get engaged and accomplish more than you anticipated? Or, did you just keep reading? Do yourself a favor; include a few minutes on the stuff that is important to you regularly. You will build a *do it muscle* that will grow stronger as you exercise it. You will also discover that the doing was not nearly as difficult as you anticipated.

Once you have primed the pump with a little action, you can lay out a game plan and some contingency strategies. Enlist the support of a friend or a thing to keep you on point. Set an alarm or arrange a friendly "get started" reminder from a colleague. Use what works for you. Remind yourself why it is important to you. If it feels insurmountable break it down into small projects and chart it.

Your passion can be made manifest much like a building is constructed. You have the vision; you make a decision. You capture it on paper. Your blueprint is carried out by experts you enlist, and you oversee the job for accuracy and clarity of interpretation. Try it. Try it on

IF YOU CAN'T CALM THE WATERS, LEARN TO RIDE THE WAVES
Clifton Anthony McKnight

something tangible to you now and gather some momentum.

Dr. Mary McKnight-Taylor was "Mom" long before she continued her education to become an educator. Her struggles and successes began long before then. Nonetheless, from an intimate perspective, my brother and I watched Mom operate with grace and struggle as a divorced single parent to raise us while pursing a better future through higher education.

The die was cast and Mother determined that the best direction for her to take her family to a better tomorrow was to pursue her education. My brother and I watched Mom obtain a bachelor's degree while working a variety of often menial part-time and full-time jobs. We saw Mom earn her M.Ed. and her Ed. D. During this pilgrimage, she would lose both her mother and father.

Shortly after, Mom remarried and would go on to survive the passing of her husband and my step-father, William Roscoe Taylor, Jr. More recently, she would endure the passing of her "baby sister" Thelma Minion. You may recall a quote proffered from my aunt early in this book. Dr. Mom offers the following insights to you in a more straightforward format.

Interview - Mary McKnight-Taylor Ed.D.

> I consider myself to be resilient. Although much in my childhood history remains painful even today, I am not consumed by wishful thinking about how it could have been.

IF YOU CAN'T CALM THE WATERS, LEARN TO RIDE THE WAVES

Clifton Anthony McKnight

I try to live as The Serenity Prayer suggests. "Lord, grant me the serenity to accept the things I cannot change; courage to change the things I can; and wisdom to know the difference..." Listed below are some factors of resilient persons:

1. A strong sense of self efficacy, a feeling that they CAN perform well, even if their current efforts have fallen short of their goal or failed.
2. At least one positive, supportive, adult figure in their lives, not necessarily in their day to day functioning, but someone who is available for emotional support, or advice and guidance in problem solving or goal setting.
3. A sense of humor
4. A social network of peers
5. Self discipline
6. Empathy-the ability to experience the feelings of others
7. Realistic interpretation of their current circumstances while remaining optimistic that those circumstances may change in a positive direction
8. The ability to remain positive in the face of only modest returns for extraordinary efforts
9. An understanding that to some extent, their action or inaction is responsible for outcomes
10. Experience some success in relationships with peers and adults. ✧

Dr. McKnight-Taylor had set her sails toward a better world through higher education that would change the lives of her children and reverberate through the many lives she would touch teaching graduate courses

How to Succeed in Turbulent Times

IF YOU CAN'T CALM THE WATERS, LEARN TO RIDE THE WAVES
Clifton Anthony McKnight

and working with Head Start programs, outreach programs, and exceptional children. Dr. McKnight-Taylor, Mom, would also become a model of possibility for me.

STAR - Sayings, Thoughts, Actions, Resources

Sayings

"*Most of the things worth doing in the world had been declared impossible before they were done.*"
- Louis D. Brandeis

"*What matters, therefore, is not the meaning of life in general, but rather, the specific meaning of a person's life at a given moment.*" - Viktor Frankl

"*Find your voice and help others to find theirs.*"
- Dr. Stephen Covey

Thoughts

"*Get intimate with your path. Learn the nooks and crannies, the potholes and mud holes. How? Think about it all the time. Practice, do. Ask, research, be. Study the geography of your task. Who is in it? Practice immersion... Immerse your self.*"

"*Who we desire to be and what we desire to accomplish is a choice that we had better make for ourselves because there are many people out there who would do it for us, on their terms.*"

How to Succeed in Turbulent Times

IF YOU CAN'T CALM THE WATERS, LEARN TO RIDE THE WAVES

Clifton Anthony McKnight

"Reserve your right to choose. It is a human inheritance that deserves embrace in a deliberate way. We are responsible, 'response able' when we consciously choose."

"Anything that moves you forward is moving you forward. You have the vision; you make the decision."

— Clif McKnight

Actions

1. Take the simple action of consciously and vocally declaring what you want and what deliberate actions you intend to take.
2. Write the plan. Create the images.
3. Begin now. Before you read another page, do one more thing toward your vision.
4. Clarify it and take at least one deliberate action towards achieving it.
5. Review Dr. McKnight-Taylor's 10 characteristics of a resilient person. How closely does this mesh with your self-assessment? How will you use this?

Resources

Kung fu Panda – Movie

"Black Enterprise Magazine," March 2002 – Tavis Smiley

The Eighth Habit – Dr. Stephen Covey

Thriving on Chaos – Dr. Tom Peters

How to Succeed in Turbulent Times

IF YOU CAN'T CALM THE WATERS, LEARN TO RIDE THE WAVES

Clifton Anthony McKnight

Chapter Eight

Getting Others Involved With Your Success

"Teamwork makes the dream work." - *John C. Maxwell*

Getting others involved in your dreams and goals and day to day musings can be an absolute power move. So many wonderful possibilities begin to surface when we invoke the Interconnection aspect of the "Will of Fortune discussed in Chapter 2 underlying this process.

To team up with people who have expertise in areas you do not gives you immediate access to wisdom, knowledge, experience, and even power beyond your present scope. If you understand and appreciate others, you will find people looking for ways to help you. Operate in a spirit of reciprocity, and people will flock to your door to be of assistance.

What makes this especially exciting is that, in this 21st century, we are able to tap in to human resources across space via technology. Transportation and communication brings global connection within our reach. We even have the capacity to reach across time. Recording in all its various forms give us access to insights from times past. We can gain insight into ourselves through some of the great minds of our past. Revisit the Chapter 2 to remind yourself of the resource value of interconnection.

Involving others also produces that potential for synergy, enthusiasm, collegiality, and friendship. If we are to journey, let us journey with a healthy dosage of lightheartedness and joy to balance the many challenges that come before us. It will serve us well as a rejuvenating element.

"A merry heart doeth good like a medicine." This quote from Proverbs 17:22 of the King James Version of the Bible underscores the value of good natured fun. Use it liberally and frequently. Support and encourage others' success, and you will soon see others rally to assist in yours. Even if support does not come from those you supported, you will have set the trend and you will surely benefit. When you help others, you open yourself up to receive help.

Even Before You Go To "Sea" (See), You Can Begin To Make Your Net Work

As you continue to practice relaxation and to practice focusing on those things that lighten your load, albeit temporarily, you will begin to have moments of clarity and inspiration. At your next opportunity, pick up a recorder or even a portable pad so you can jot these messages or thoughts down. If you are inclined and you

IF YOU CAN'T CALM THE WATERS, LEARN TO RIDE THE WAVES
Clifton Anthony McKnight

have a mobile phone, you can text or email yourself a message and save it for later review.

What a world! It is amazing how inspirations can "just show up" when we are in a relaxed state of mind. And you will be amazed at the people you attract when you are positive and relaxed. You may not have given yourself the privilege of meditating on your life's purpose or on a plan for living, yet thinking well of others and acting on those thoughts the "net" in network begins to come together.

It is sort of like an extension of faith. I was brought up with the powerful message from Matthew 17:20 in the Bible who, in admonishing his disciples regarding their lack of faith, spoke of the power of faith, "And Jesus said unto them, Because of your unbelief: for verily I say unto you, If ye have faith as a grain of mustard seed, ye shall say unto this mountain, Remove hence to yonder place; and it shall remove; and nothing shall be impossible unto you." Consider visiting your spiritual work, and see what else you can find that addresses this premise. People rise above their best for the individual who displays genuine faith in them and speaks well of them.

Even before your plan is in place by thinking well of others, your team begins to form. When you feel good about another, generally you initiate a ripple effect which ultimately leads back to warm thoughts about you. People that you may yet to have met begin to be indirectly led to you by the words and thoughts of those you touch.

How to Succeed in Turbulent Times

IF YOU CAN'T CALM THE WATERS, LEARN TO RIDE THE WAVES

Clifton Anthony McKnight

Help Paddle Someone Else's Boat

What a splendid concept this is. Take your eyes off you and focus on making someone else's day, goal, dream come alive. Helping others solve their problems allows them to experience empowerment while also experiencing connection, community, and comfort.

Something happens to you, too. Your problems are no longer a focal point, freeing your creative juices from the paralysis of fear and worry. Your hopes and dreams begin to gestate since you are not anxiously and prematurely pulling up the desired end to inspect the roots. Without a doubt, working toward the benefit of others serves the server as well.

On still another level, you are experiencing the joy that comes with making the world a better place. You have helped someone live well. Remember how it feels to see the joy on someone's face, knowing that you put it there? Think back and re-experience it. Great feeling, isn't it? You can visit that memory and sit there long enough to put a BIG smile on your own face AND you can do it again for someone else. Mahatma Gandhi said, "Be the Change you want to see in the world."

Do what you can, when you can, for who you can, while you can. When you want to see a difference, simply be the difference. Don't take it on as obligation, for the blessings are diminished when you operate out of burden.

I saw the actor Will Smith on the *Oprah Show* one evening. Yep, I am referencing the *Oprah Show* again. Sabbatical was nice, and wherever I see value, I accept it if

IF YOU CAN'T CALM THE WATERS, LEARN TO RIDE THE WAVES
Clifton Anthony McKnight

I can. Anyway, Will said a few things that really resonated with me that I believe you will appreciate as well. He said, "The only way to truly be happy is to be in service to humanity." Now, I don't know if it is the *only* way, but without a doubt it certainly is one way.

Will also knocked the cover off the ball for me when he said, "Your life will become better by making someone else's [life] better." Go online and check it out for yourself. It was on *The Oprah Winfrey Show*, Wednesday, December 17, 2008.

Think Bridges

Think about it. The more we sow, the greater the harvest. To boot, the yield is exponential in its returns. When others build walls, we can build bridges. Bridges allow us to reach over obstacles and discover new possibilities.

Emotional walls are often built to protect. The problem is that we ostensibly cut ourselves off from the greater gifts, the experience of relationship, and the experience of interconnection. We remain a part of existence; we are very much connected, but we are no longer aware of the fruits from it. It's like having a million dollars in the bank and being unaware that you have it. You couldn't put it to use.

Cutting ourselves off from something can indeed be a survival mechanism. Sometimes, all we can do is to compartmentalize those things that are deeply traumatic

IF YOU CAN'T CALM THE WATERS, LEARN TO RIDE THE WAVES

Clifton Anthony McKnight

while we try to make sense of life and our previous construct. The only problem I have with this thought is that too often we stop at the separation stage. If one is not mindful, setting up an emotional fortress can result in arrested development. Give yourself the occasional "Checkup from the neck up." Contemplate and communicate with a loved one. Meditate and pray. "Think Bridges."

Likely, when there is pain or struggle, we are on the precipice of a quantum leap. Your life is preparing you for a new beginning, a rebirth, if you will. Will Smith said something else I liked, and it really fits nicely with the "Will of Fortune." He said that we tend to think of life much like a linear timeline: we are born, we live, and we die. He suggests that we bend the timeline into a circle by connecting one end to the other.

We are born, we live life; there is death and then there is rebirth. You learn a skill and get a job (birth), lose the job (death), find a better scenario, start a business or get a better job (rebirth). As time passes, people may separate from one another, move, divorce, or someone passes. Eventually, new relationships are formed and new experiences forged, only now, you carry the wisdom from your previous life .

Remember, your history alone does not determine where you are or who you are. How you decide to use that history contributes to new bridges of possibility. External factors also can make a difference. Be sure to reserve the privilege of interpreting your own path. Decide for yourself how you will be in the face of

How to Succeed in Turbulent Times

IF YOU CAN'T CALM THE WATERS, LEARN TO RIDE THE WAVES

Clifton Anthony McKnight

adversity and opportunity. Hold fast to your dreams, and the next rebirth will manifest them. Like the cab driver, ticket agent, or that old Microsoft ® commercial might say, "Where do you want to go today?"

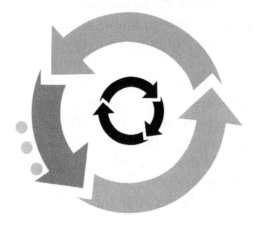

Upon rebirth we find we are more than we were before, and whatever the new living looks like it stands to offer, still newer fruits that we may enjoy. One door closes, another opens. We are more equipped when it does. The intensity of these experiences is made manageable when we grasp from a spiritual perspective, a timeless perspective.

IF YOU CAN'T CALM THE WATERS, LEARN TO RIDE THE WAVES

Clifton Anthony McKnight

We graduate from school and that experience passes on and gives birth to a new experience. We call it work; or if we worked while at school, maybe we begin a career, thus a new career is born. Even if it is continued education in a new institution, we are introduced to a new set of relationships and a new space for learning. In these terms, we can acknowledge rebirth within this single existence. Let go and be born again.

How to Succeed in Turbulent Times

IF YOU CAN'T CALM THE WATERS, LEARN TO RIDE THE WAVES
Clifton Anthony McKnight

Are you waking up to technology? Might you be motivated to be better today than you were yesterday? Join the rest of the world. We all have areas in need of fortification based on our own desires. And it doesn't matter where you begin. It only matters that you begin.

"Today 'is' because of what yesterday was and tomorrow will be what we produce in the thoughts and actions of today. " The people you serve today may be of service to the people who can help you tomorrow. More directly, they can be the people who serve you tomorrow. We are all connected. Take a look at what Michael Thomas had to say. Michael has been renowned to have helped literally hundreds of first generation college graduates to attend and complete college. The following interview was augmented by additional conversations.

Interview – Michael Thomas M.B.A

> *Mike:* At age 13, I went to work for a United States Congressman. High expectations were set for me back then. I have always had the mindset that I would continue to promote the banner of high expectations to others. I grew up hearing leaders say, "You are somebody… "
>
> I am very interested in the Lumina Foundation – national effort to strengthen community college students (Achieving The Dream). Their efforts are focused on a much deserving population.
>
> *Clif:* What happened (or is happening)?

How to Succeed in Turbulent Times

IF YOU CAN'T CALM THE WATERS, LEARN TO RIDE THE WAVES

Clifton Anthony McKnight

Mike: Life challenges still happen. One of the greatest adjustments in my life occurred in 1987. My wife suffered an injury that changed our lives forever. She went to work healthy one day and came home a week later a different person.

My wife was left with reflex sympathetic dystrophy. She lost the use of most of her right leg, and her entire nervous system was affected.

I was focused on corporate America when this injury happened to my wife. I had to make some tough choices, injury wife and we had 2 small children in tow. A challenging experience like this can make you lose your way. Financial challenges began to mushroom after staying home, taking care of wife and two small children. The positive side of tribulation is that you bounce back, having learned something, if you are thinking and reflecting on the right issues: family.

Also, giving me challenges is the fact that Detroit is hit particularly hard with this economic downturn. Education is a challenge for the unemployed and underprepared college student. People have to remember, it started here in Detroit long before the country felt the effect on its economy. It has been a struggle to help students achieve their goal of obtaining a degree.

Clif: How are you?

How to Succeed in Turbulent Times

IF YOU CAN'T CALM THE WATERS, LEARN TO RIDE THE WAVES

Clifton Anthony McKnight

Mike: I am better than most around me. I stayed in Detroit when others moved out. I am not so much concerned about myself as for my neighbors and community. Some of that concern for others is the shift I made when my wife was injured. I am clear that some things are simply beyond my control; however, I should do everything in my control to make things better for others.

If my family is good, I am good. I will continue to do fine. I am not one to complain. How can I complain? I have not been directly impacted with major bad situations like some others.

Clif: How do you or, how did you, manage?

Mike: Sometimes, I just need to sit and reflect. Langston Hughes wrote, "Life ain't been no crystal stair." Still, I recognize that I do not have a right to whine. My grandparents had it worse. My parents had it worse than I. I know that others have it worse. I work with them every term trying to get them to see education is a way UP.

I think of those who came before me. I can do no less for mine than what was done for me.

It wasn't easy at first. I had a strong understanding that I knew I had to make it and get through tough situations.

IF YOU CAN'T CALM THE WATERS, LEARN TO RIDE THE WAVES

Clifton Anthony McKnight

How did I manage? Faith in my education, experiences, and skills ... We had 2 children. I was in my 20's. My children and wife looked to me for leadership and direction. I had to show up in the household with my A game. Shift from employment goals to household goals, placing my employment goals on hold for a while. Faith helps me defer my direction to maintain a working household.

Clif: What have you learned?

Mike: Faith, education, and hope will help us weather any storms.

I can recall the time during my family challenges when I was at a program in my church. My kids were performing in some play when the pastor came and sat next to me. Dr. Fredrick Sampson, the pastor, would sit or talk with me to make sure I was staying strong. This evening, he said something to me that I will never forget. He said:

> I believe we owe our children something;
>
> 1. The first thing is to make them smart;
>
> 2 Teach them character;
>
> 3 Create opportunities for them by removing barriers;

How to Succeed in Turbulent Times

IF YOU CAN'T CALM THE WATERS, LEARN TO RIDE THE WAVES
Clifton Anthony McKnight

4. Expose them to religion for the unforeseen because it will help them survive the storms that will invariably come.

The last thing Dr. Rev Sampson said to me was to:

Remember that everybody you meet is somebody's child.

That last statement changed my thinking, focus, and as I sometimes joke, messed me up. I have committed many days attempting to make people smart, teach the character, remove barriers, and create opportunities. And, expose them to a high power to help them through the storms.

Clif: What suggestions do you have for others?

Mike: Let us work to make children (individuals) smart. When one comes to see you (or seek your help) ,do what you can to have them leave satisfied. Find one reason to assist them. Of course, we can all find reasons not to help others, but the real challenge is to find one, just one reason to help somebody.

My son and daughter are continuing the legacy of helping others. All our sons and daughter can do the same. Let us create a snowball effect developing character, making them smart, teaching them to create opportunities.

Clif: What else would you like to say?

IF YOU CAN'T CALM THE WATERS, LEARN TO RIDE THE WAVES
Clifton Anthony McKnight

Mike: Someone helped me. Someone did these things for me. I am a first generation college graduate. Today, both of my children graduated from college. I have a great respect for life and education.

Clif: So, we can just keep "Paying it forward." ✧

Remember: "It comes to pass." It doesn't come to stay. Live, love, create, and have fun. Be good to yourself and to one another. Visit www.motivision.net (that's "**.net**") and start your day with a little love and possibility and maybe sign up for a "Motive Vision Moment." Drop a note sometime, and let me know of your struggles and your victories. Even better, drop a loved one a note and bless them with a personal uplifting message. My suggestion to you is embodied in a short poem I recently penned;

Hold True to Yourself

Live fully today, in work in love in play.
Embrace positive possibility and opportunity flourishes.
Give in to fears and anxiety appears.
See the Good with heartfelt praise.
More joy, more peace, more love we raise.
Share if you dare. Have a care but don't despair.
Hold true to your self and your vision will prepare.
Hold true to your self and if you listen, you will hear.
  – Clif McKnight

Remember, kindness and love are like perfume…
  – Clifton A. McKnight

How to Succeed in Turbulent Times

IF YOU CAN'T CALM THE WATERS, LEARN TO RIDE THE WAVES
Clifton Anthony McKnight

STAR
Sayings

"Teamwork makes the dream work." – *John C Maxwell*

"Do what you can, when you can, for who you can, while you can." Clif McKnight

"Be the Change you want to see in the world." - *Gandhi*

"Where do you want to go today?"

"A merry heart doeth good like a medicine." - Proverbs 17:22, Bible, King James Version

Thoughts

"When you want to see a difference, be the difference."

"Give yourself a "Check up from the neck up."

"One door closes, another opens."

"Let go and be born again." - Clif McKnight

"What matters, therefore, is not the meaning of life in general, but rather, the specific meaning of a person's life at a given moment."
— Viktor Frankl

IF YOU CAN'T CALM THE WATERS, LEARN TO RIDE THE WAVES

Clifton Anthony McKnight

Actions

1. Look in your spiritual text for reference to faith and love for others to strengthen your perspective.
2. Make a list of 10 people you know and what you love about them. At your earliest opportunity, communicate that to them. A brief phone call, an email, or even a text message can make a difference in their lives... and yours.
3. Ask yourself, "How will I be reborn?" and create the space to listen for the answer.
4. Dedicate some time, money, prayer, or other resource toward a cause or charity of your choice. Consider doing this today, even if you already do this.
5. Consider a relationship that has been damaged and take some action towards its mending without attaching yourself to an outcome. The action is as much for your healing as it is for the other person.

Resources

Man's Search for Meaning - Viktor Frankl

Six Degrees of Separation – http://www.sixdegrees.org/

A Long Way Gone, Memoirs Of A Boy Soldier – Ishmael Beal

Teamwork Makes The Dream Work - John C. Maxwell

Pay it Forward - Movie

How to Succeed in Turbulent Times

Chapter Nine

Prosperity, the Beginning

"One must discover their inner self... Find that oneness or unity with the Divine Source and you find the Christ within you."

– Ian Grant, M.D

Cultivating "Prosperity Consciousness"

*L**ife does not end, it just ushers in a new beginning.* **To recognize this is a step in Prosperity consciousness.** When times are hard, we have but to remind ourselves that "This too shall pass" <u>AND</u> that there are opportunities in the midst of the struggle. Looking for the lessons in the struggle positions us for something new and better even if it is but a new and better perspective.

The path of prosperity is lined with prayer and introspection, purpose that recognizes our mutuality, personal relationships grounded with love, positive perspective (love of life), peace through comfort in

IF YOU CAN'T CALM THE WATERS, LEARN TO RIDE THE WAVES

Clifton Anthony McKnight

stillness, and financial prosperity--defined as more coming in than going out.

When you tune in to prosperity, insightful and inspirational remnants may be discovered virtually anywhere. How do you do this? Open your eyes and you will see prosperity in nature. This is principle. Years ago, I heard a seminar speaker named Jim Brooks ask, "How many apple seeds are in an apple? How many apples are in a seed?" If you consider the apple trees that are born from a single apple and the many apples in each tree with seeds in them as well, you may begin to get the picture. How many apples are in a seed? Orchards and orchards are in a single seed that realizes it's potential. It is all in how you think.

Though I first heard that analogy decades ago, I see semblance of it everywhere. Think in terms of all you presently have, imagine from whence it all came, and operate from there. Be full of gratitude, and watch your territory continue to enlarge. Your capacity is immense. You are born from 2 who were each born from 2 and those 4 were each born from 2. Even if we stop around that level, when you include the parents, the energy of around 30 ancestors have combined to manifest you. You have something to say, and you have something to accomplish.

The process or principles of prosperity are consistent whether we refer to relationships, spirituality, health, or finance. To paraphrase my good friend **Ian Grant, M.D.,** "One must discover their inner self... Find

IF YOU CAN'T CALM THE WATERS, LEARN TO RIDE THE WAVES
Clifton Anthony McKnight

that oneness or unity with the Divine Source and you find the Christ within you." Adjust your focus and your efforts, and watch your territory grow.

As long as you remain in the question, you can draw from within and from others. Just be certain to reserve at all times the authority to ultimately choose and interpret for yourself. That is, let no individual move you from what your spirit intuits. Explore what others have to say. Observe the fruit on their trees. Gauge and adjust until you recognize the customized road you have to travel.

Sure, you can ask for a piece of someone else's pie. You can also obtain or create a recipe and bake your own pie. Usually, the best pies come with a little help or a lot of experience. Choose your strategy, and shake and bake. The key is to choose.

You can choose to hoard and hide, or you can elect to share and ride. The more you give, the more you are likely to receive. First of all, you will have made room to receive, and secondly, you inspire a splendid chain reaction of kindness. Prosperity is yours, indeed.

There are many measures for success. The smart thing, in my opinion, is for each of us to establish Our own definition. Consider this quote by Ralph Waldo Emerson:

Success
"How do you measure success?
To laugh often and much
To win the respect of intelligent people

How to Succeed in Turbulent Times

IF YOU CAN'T CALM THE WATERS, LEARN TO RIDE THE WAVES
Clifton Anthony McKnight

And the affection of children;
To earn the appreciation of honest critics
And endure the betrayal of false friends;
To appreciate beauty;
To find the best in others;
To leave the world a bit better,
Whether by a healthy child, a garden patch,
A redeemed social condition or a job well done;
To know even one other life has breathed easier
Because you have lived -
This is to succeed."

Finances

So, what is there to talk about regarding finances? You only have to follow the direction of the thoughts in this book to roll where I am headed. Set your sails in the right direction. Resolve to make each week more profitable for the household, for the business, etc. Put systems in place to keep at least a little bit of what you earn whenever you earn, and put it to work for you. Fredric Lehrman suggests the following mantra in his series on "Prosperity Consciousness": "A part of all I earn is mine to keep." It is a worthy affirmation.

Consider setting up separate accounts for specific purposes. Lehrman suggests an account for major purchases and one for bills and one for guiltless spending (my words I think), among others. Choose how and where or even if this might work for you. Carefully consider the observations and verifiable experiences of others who have gone where you desire to go.

How to Succeed in Turbulent Times

IF YOU CAN'T CALM THE WATERS, LEARN TO RIDE THE WAVES

Clifton Anthony McKnight

Educate, educate, educate. The more you learn about finances, the more you will have to work with for financial planning and crisis prevention. The resources are over-running. Learn about assets, things that earn money for you, and liabilities, things that cost you money. Explore how assets can work for you as opposed to your only having *you* to work for you. Have you had a downturn where some assets have degraded into liabilities? Don't give up; get your check up from the neck up and learn more. Watch successful people who are doing what you would like to do, and customize what you observe to fit you.

Stocks, options, foreign exchange, businesses, and real estate are just a few examples of potential assets worthy of your attention. While you explore and experiment, please remember the simple math and the value of compounding. Even a low-paying savings account compounds when regular contributions are made over time. I read about an 80+ year old woman who washed clothes for a living all of her life out of Mississippi. She donated over 1 million dollars to a university there. She was able to accumulate so much money by keeping a portion of what she earned over the years. Nothing fancy, just hold some and keep adding, and get some kind of interest rate. Read about icons such as Warren Buffet, consider his philosophy as well as others, and render your own decisions.

Look up online the rule of 72 which allows one to calculate how long it will take for your money to double based on the number 72 divided by the interest rate.

How to Succeed in Turbulent Times

IF YOU CAN'T CALM THE WATERS, LEARN TO RIDE THE WAVES
Clifton Anthony McKnight

Example: 72 divided by 9% interest rate = 8 years (8x9= 72) or if interest rate is 6%, 72 divided by 6% = 12 years (6 x 12 = 72) etc. How is this useful? You decide. Perhaps it can help you project earnings from your deposits over time or inspire you to explore multiple avenues.

Be aware that compound interest can also work against you. High interest debt such as credit card debt can leave you owing years of payments for that sale item you just could not pass up. I found out the hard way that the best use of a credit card is to pay it off in full prior to the cycle date, sometimes 30 days, or 28 days, or whatever is noted in the fine print.

Compounding to some is the tortoise, and instruments such as options trading and real estate investment may represent the hare. Even in the midst of the housing slump, I recommend that you explore carefully the world of real estate and the world of stocks, bonds, and other financial instruments. If you buy when the prices for assets are down, there is still risk, but there is also great opportunity.

Of course, there are many elements to consider as you explore this. Read, learn, simulate. Keep in mind that an asset is intended to generate positive income. When it is not contributing to your prosperity, then it is not at that time an asset.

My father-in-law, Carlton Burke, is a very strong buy and hold kind of guy. He has effectively demonstrated to me that if you hold real estate long enough and you structure your finances so that it is not a burden, even if it is not an asset in the sense that it is not

IF YOU CAN'T CALM THE WATERS, LEARN TO RIDE THE WAVES
Clifton Anthony McKnight

bringing you money in the moment, it can very well play out as an asset inasmuch as the ultimate value at liquidation can dwarf most savings instruments known to the populace.

Consider learning from others in classes, workshops. Have conversations with people who are successful at what you are interested in considering, and test the waters on paper only for awhile. When you feel ready, invest only what you can afford to lose in the beginning or jump on in based on your risk tolerance. Wealth creation proponents strongly recommend including the services of an accountant, book-keeper and lawyer as you create your system for wealth development. Bankers and financial planners can round things out for you to be sure the process for selecting the proper individuals for your team will depend on you and your style, needs, and resources.

If you are genuinely interested in maximizing your finances, don't try to be spoon fed. Examine, practice, examine some more, and prepare for a ride filled with twists and turns. And if you are downsized, laid off, riffed, or just self-motivated, even in this economic climate, particularly in this economic climate, I suggest that you investigate the feasibility of starting a business or helping others to start theirs (hmmm sound like a business idea?).

Many resources and possibilities are at your fingertips to help you get started. Visit the websites and blogs of business magazines like *Entrepreneur Magazine* and *Black Enterprise Magazine*. Business and finance is

IF YOU CAN'T CALM THE WATERS, LEARN TO RIDE THE WAVES

Clifton Anthony McKnight

green; don't be dissuaded if you are not Black or African American. Great information and inspiration can be found there. Visit other specialty sites as well. Visit government websites like www.sba.gov and http://business.gov/start/index.html . Visit my blog http://www.harebrainedebusinesses.blogspot.com It is "freakin' amazing" what is available. Start today.

One final thought about compounding. Compounding is a principle. It applies to virtually everything in life. In learning, laughing, loving, and living, compounding occurs. Regular deposits of fun incur *interest* that make you a more fun person. Each action makes the next more easy until it becomes automatic. It is even bigger than that! Compounding thoughts don't just make it easier to perpetuate the same thought they lead to actions and it continues. Many years ago I heard a saying whose sentiment has been with me ever since. You may have heard it yourself. I believe it paraphrases an Emerson quote. It is as follows:

>Sow a Thought, Reap an Action
>Sow an Action, Reap a Habit
>Sow a Habit, Reap a Character
>Sow a Character, Reap a Destiny

It all begins with cultivated thought. Read it over a few times, and really think on it. You just may add more spice to your life.

IF YOU CAN'T CALM THE WATERS, LEARN TO RIDE THE WAVES

Clifton Anthony McKnight

Oceans, Sunshine and Rain - The Inner self and other Gifts that Money Can't Buy

Let's face it. Life is full of ups and downs, ins and outs, comings and goings, wet spells, dry spells, calm waters, choppy waters, clear skies, fierce storms, sunshine and rain. The list goes on. We ride the waves, and sometimes we take in a little water. Sometimes, we need CPR!

As often as you can, remember how nature makes the most of things and how waters flow. There is ebb, and there is flow. Sun is good, and too much can burn. Rain is essential to growth. See the beauty in it all. Even if it is only the contrast and the memory of better days and anticipation of days to come, it can serve you.

You can also learn to anticipate and establish contingencies for the inevitable shifts and changes. They are pretty much guaranteed to occur in all things life brings. You may remember the song/verse/saying, "To everything there is a season..." It might surprise some of you to know that this is part of a Bible passage in Ecclesiastes 3:1.

According to a study conducted by the American Psychological Association, stress levels have increased dramatically in 2008 from 2007. (in a press release dated October 7, 2008, 9:00 a.m. EDT). Among other things, the study indicates that 8 out of 10 Americans indicate that they are stressed about the economy.

For many, it has only gotten worse. With women serving as primary caregivers at home, the stress level of

IF YOU CAN'T CALM THE WATERS, LEARN TO RIDE THE WAVES

Clifton Anthony McKnight

raising and caring for children while tending to an elderly relative suggests that the plot sickens. In fact in every category that I read the percentage of women reporting being stressed was greater than for men. We have to relax more. Ladies, give yourself permission. If the vehicle breaks down, no one rides and in many cases, guess who the vehicle is?

Umm fellas, this goes for you, too. It seems to me that more women are inclined to have that Spa day than men. Okay, okay, we have other ways of letting off steam, a good game, playing or "spectating," a good laugh, a game of cards or what ever it is (massage maybe?) go for it. No gender roles. Do what you do... "Do you," as a popular artist says.

When the waters are calm and the sun is out, if you are on a yacht, cruise ship, or sailboat, you take a moment, relax, and just enjoy it. If you really want to maximize your experiences in life, learn to RELAX during the storm as well. When you are at home, a rain storm is a great time to relax by the fire, in the bed, on the couch, whatever. Read, sleep; talk to a close friend. Catch a movie. Work on something that requires your attention that you may have been putting off.

How much is this a metaphor for life? When things are most challenging and there is nothing you can do, when the "rain is coming down," what better things are there but relaxation and focus or talking with a loved one or getting something done that has been "hounding" you. REMEMBER, "Everywhere you go, there you are." Yeah, I feel like Yogi Bearer. The sweet simple truth is

How to Succeed in Turbulent Times

IF YOU CAN'T CALM THE WATERS, LEARN TO RIDE THE WAVES
Clifton Anthony McKnight

that within you can find just about anything, and you can take yourself where you need to, when you need to! Sometimes, to influence your internal self, it helps to find an external environment that stimulates where you want to go mentally.

The splendid thing in life is that the converse is also true. To influence your environment, you create an internal stimulus that calls you to create or locate the external reality you desire. *We are offspring and architects of Prosperity! We create what we want. We create what we don't. Either way, we prosper at the creating.*

Here are a four strategies you can use to attract prosperity, whatever it is that represents prosperity for you: 1] Identify the playing field and dedicate your attention to it; 2] Choose a field where you are filled; 3] Study others who have prospered in or on that field in person where feasible and through literature and other resources when not feasible; 4] <u>Play</u> on that field. Even while you learn, have fun with it.

"Build a Better Tomorrow, Today"

How we live manifests our legacy. We can organize our lives so that we can contribute to the building of a hospital or clinic that saves lives well into the future. It could be a legacy born from the love and tutelage of a son or daughter who embraces those teachings and becomes a shining possibility for the future. Legacy can also be the loving advice or encouraging hand we provide to someone that

IF YOU CAN'T CALM THE WATERS, LEARN TO RIDE THE WAVES

Clifton Anthony McKnight

is later inspired to build a chain of clinics to serve the less fortunate. A better tomorrow might be stimulated by helping someone who is inspired by that help to assist two others who are inspired to help many more who… and the ripple continues.

"Interview" Bob Parsons, Founder, of GoDaddy.com

Technology made it possible for me to share the insights of online website guru Bob Parsons without ever corresponding with him or even meeting him. What is available to you and to me in the 21st century can contribute immensely to your riding the waves.

Bob Parsons was born in Baltimore, Maryland, the same city where my brother and I were raised. Interestingly, Bob was brought up in a lower middle class family and during his early years was less than accomplished in school. Financially, according to his blog, "We were always broke."

Bob's choices lead him far away from mediocrity to a place where he owns multiple interests, including Godaddy.com, a leading web domain registry and website servicing company. *The following represents 16 "rules for success in business and life in general," delineated by Bob Parsons, Founder, of GoDaddy.com.*

1. Get out of your comfort zone often. I believe that not much happens of any significance when we're in our comfort zone. I hear people say, "But I'm concerned about security." My response to that is simple: "Security is for

IF YOU CAN'T CALM THE WATERS, LEARN TO RIDE THE WAVES
Clifton Anthony McKnight

cadavers." After stretching awhile, you can relax and enjoy "the fruits of your labor."

2. Never give up. Almost nothing works the first time it's attempted. Just because what you're doing does not seem to be working, doesn't mean it won't work. It just means that it might not work the way you're doing it. If it was easy, everyone would be doing it, and you wouldn't have an opportunity.

3. When you're ready to quit, you're closer than you think. There's an old Chinese saying that I just love, and I believe it is so true. It goes like this: "The temptation to quit will be greatest just before you are about to succeed."

4. With regard to whatever worries you, not only accept the worst thing that could happen, but make it a point to quantify what the worst thing could be. Very seldom will the worst consequence be anywhere near as bad as a cloud of "undefined consequences." My father would tell me early on, when I was struggling and losing my shirt trying to get Parsons Technology going, "Well, Robert, if it doesn't work, they can't eat you."

5. Focus on what you want to have happen. Remember that old saying, "As you think, so shall you be."

6. Take things a day at a time. No matter how difficult your situation is, you can get through it if you don't look too far into the future, and focus on the present moment. You can get through anything one day at a time.

7. Always be moving forward. Never stop investing. Never

IF YOU CAN'T CALM THE WATERS, LEARN TO RIDE THE WAVES

Clifton Anthony McKnight

stop improving. Never stop doing something new. The moment you stop improving your organization, it starts to die. Make it your goal to be better each and every day, in some small way. Remember the Japanese concept of Kaizen. Small daily improvements eventually result in huge advantages.

8. Be quick to decide. Remember what General George S. Patton said: "A good plan violently executed today is far and away better than a perfect plan tomorrow."

9. Measure everything of significance. I swear this is true. Anything that is measured and watched, improves.

10. Anything that is not managed will deteriorate. If you want to uncover problems you don't know about, take a few moments and look closely at the areas you haven't examined for a while. I guarantee you problems will be there.

11. Pay attention to your competitors, but pay more attention to what you're doing. When you look at your competitors, remember that everything looks perfect at a distance. Even the planet Earth, if you get far enough into space, looks like a peaceful place.

12. Never let anybody push you around. In our society, with our laws and even playing field, you have just as much right to what you're doing as anyone else, provided that what you're doing is legal.

13. Never expect life to be fair. Life isn't fair. You make your own breaks. You'll be doing good if the only meaning

IF YOU CAN'T CALM THE WATERS, LEARN TO RIDE THE WAVES

Clifton Anthony McKnight

fair has to you, is something that you pay when you get on a bus (i.e., fare).

14. Solve your own problems. You'll find that by coming up with your own solutions, you'll develop a competitive edge. Masura Ibuka, the co-founder of SONY, said it best: "You never succeed in technology, business, or anything by following the others." There's also an old Asian saying that I remind myself of frequently. It goes like this: "A wise man keeps his own counsel."

15. Don't take yourself too seriously. Lighten up. Often, at least half of what we accomplish is due to luck. None of us are in control as much as we like to think we are.

16. There's always a reason to smile. Find it. After all, you're really lucky just to be alive. Life is short. More and more, I agree with my little brother. He always reminds me: "We're not here for a long time; we're here for a good time."

The above "Rules for Survival" is included with the permission of Bob Parsons (http://www.bobparsons.com) and is Copyright © 2004-2006 by Bob Parsons. All rights reserved. ✧

His comments may carry a different tone than my writings as well as of those whom I have interviewed. Yet, some of the messages are the same. Persistence, darkest before the dawn, keeping it light, and carry a positive attitude all showed up for me. Did you catch it?

Congratulations! By now you probably have a real appreciation that you have made it to – the beginning. If not please go back and read the previous chapter. Now

How to Succeed in Turbulent Times

IF YOU CAN'T CALM THE WATERS, LEARN TO RIDE THE WAVES
Clifton Anthony McKnight

all you have to do is celebrate the ups and seek to understand the downs, or at the least, broaden your perspective regarding the downs so that the lessons may serve. Then take hold of the passion within and be the difference.

Please, stay in touch with those you care about and with me too. Take the time to connect internally and appreciate all the beauty around you. Where there are troubled waters, be a beacon for possibility. The best is yet to come.

How to Succeed in Turbulent Times

IF YOU CAN'T CALM THE WATERS, LEARN TO RIDE THE WAVES

Clifton Anthony McKnight

STAR
Sayings

"There has never been a time, nor will there ever be a time, when it's not your time."

–Mark Holland

"But seek ye first the kingdom of God, and his righteousness; and all these things shall be added unto you." – Matthew 6:33 *Bible*, King James Version

> Sow a Thought, Reap an Action
> Sow an Action, Reap a Habit
> Sow a Habit, Reap a Character
> Sow a Character, Reap a Destiny

"WE are offspring and architects of Prosperity! We create what we want. We create what we don't. Either way, we prosper at the creating."

"Everywhere you go, there you are." – Clif McKnight

"To everything there is a season." - The Holy Bible Ecclesiastes 3:1.

"You are everything and everything is You." – The Stylistics

Thoughts

"Seeking the best that money can buy" is not equivalent to" Seeking the best life has to offer."

How to Succeed in Turbulent Times

IF YOU CAN'T CALM THE WATERS, LEARN TO RIDE THE WAVES

Clifton Anthony McKnight

"WE are offspring and architects of Prosperity!" We create what we want. We create what we don't. Either way, we prosper at the creating." - Clif McKnight

"Everything is on its way to somewhere." – <u>Phenomenon</u> - MOVIE

"How many seeds are in an apple? How many apples are in a seed?" - Jim Brooks

"Choose a field where you are filled." – Clif McKnight

"One must discover their inner self... Find that oneness or unity with the Divine Source and you find the Christ within you." – Ian Grant, M.D.

"You can choose to hoard and hide or you can elect to share and ride." – Clifton McKnight

"Adjust your focus and your efforts and watch your territory grow." – Clifton McKnight

Actions

1. Spend at least 15 minutes **acknowledging** the things you appreciate about yourself and your situation. If you can only squeeze 5 minutes at first, take 5.

2. List 5 things you can do today that bring you an experience of joy peace or love. Do at least 2.

How to Succeed in Turbulent Times

IF YOU CAN'T CALM THE WATERS, LEARN TO RIDE THE WAVES
Clifton Anthony McKnight

3. Identify one thing you could do immediately to add zest, peace, love, and/or joy to your day that would not interrupt anything essential or cause duress later. Please! Stop and do it NOW.

4. <u>Four strategies you can use to attract Prosperity</u>
   - ✓ Identify the playing field and dedicate your attention to it;
   - ✓ Choose a field where you are filled;
   - ✓ Study others who have prospered in or on that field in person where feasible and through literature and other resources when not feasible;
   - ✓ <u>Play</u> on that field. Even while you learn have fun with it.

Resources

Conduct an online search for fun things to do for free. Even a search can lift your spirits. At the time of this printing a few possible resources are:

http://ezinearticles.com/?Free--Fun-Things-to-Do-For-Your-Social-Life-During-the-Recession&id=1555122

http://www.thesimpledollar.com/2008/07/17/100-things-to-do-during-a-money-free-weekend/
If these links are no longer active, others are sure to present themselves.

http://www.sba.gov

IF YOU CAN'T CALM THE WATERS, LEARN TO RIDE THE WAVES
Clifton Anthony McKnight

http://business.gov/start/index.html

http://apahelpcenter.mediaroom.com/index.php?s=pageC&item=45
- American Psychological Association

Pay It Forward - Movie:

Prosperity Consciousness - Fredric Lehrman

http://cliftonmcknight.wordpress.com

www.motivision.net - Company of Clif McKnight

http://www.suzeorman.com/downloads/SuzesStory.pdf - Suzie Orman bio

Think and Grow Rich - Napoleon Hill

I Can - Ben Sweetland   I Will - Ben Sweetland

The Game of Life and How To Play it - Florence Scovell Shinn

Ageless Body Timeless Mind – Deepak Chopra M.D.

Awaken The Giant Within – Anthony Robins

7 Habits of Highly Effective People – Stephen Covey

As a Man Thinketh - James Allen

How to Succeed in Turbulent Times

IF YOU CAN'T CALM THE WATERS, LEARN TO RIDE THE WAVES
Clifton Anthony McKnight

The Last Lecture – Randy Pausch

Mitakuye Oyasin – Dr. A. C. Ross

How to Succeed in Turbulent Times

<u>IF YOU CAN'T CALM THE WATERS, LEARN TO RIDE THE WAVES</u>

Clifton Anthony McKnight

Acknowledgements

To some, it may sound cliché to say, first and foremost, I want to thank God and to some, stranger still , "the Universe," so I will take it a little bit further to offer the depth of my logic and of my appreciation. This magnificent existence is built on abundance. I say this because one cannot calculate the number of orchards that can spring from a single orange. The vastness of the universe staggers the imagination and according to our scientists continues to expand. I felt like Walt Disney's Buzz Lightyear , "To Infinity and Beyond!"(I crack myself up even if you don't get it).

In addition to deep appreciation for being in a world of such abundance (only curtailed by our human foibles and shortsightedness), I have utmost gratitude for what to me represents the LOVE of God. The gifts of FOREGIVENESS, RESILIENCE, and GRACE represent to me the offspring of Love. So, you see, it is sound and prudent and mindful to acknowledge and thank God be in gratitude with the Universe (A rose by any other name…).

I thank my nuclear family, my wife Michele, my daughters Courtney and Chelsea, and my Aunt Cynthia Tracey. I would be remiss if I did not thank the great souls AND THEIR FAMILIES who when interviewed shared their personal tribulations and triumphs in the

IF YOU CAN'T CALM THE WATERS, LEARN TO RIDE THE WAVES
Clifton Anthony McKnight

hopes that it may add to your lives. Their contributions to me go way beyond these pages. By order of "appearance," they are,

Mark Holland D.Min. – Friend, mentor, co- traveler, motivator
George Jefferson – Friend, power thinker, motivator
Elliott Marbury – Lifetime buddy, fellow seeker
Sunilda Zabala – Collegeaue, inspiration, kindred spirit
Ruth Norris – Godmother, spiritual teacher, inspiration
Maureen Edwards, Ph.D. – Colleague, spiritual giver
Mary McKnight-Taylor, Ed.D. – Mother, scholar, teacher, cheerleader
Michael Thomas, M.B.A. – Friend, colleague, bridgebuilder.

These are very special people in my life, and I would not be surprised if they take residence in your life experience by their selfless sharing in this book. You are true companions on this colorful journey. **Barbara Talley**, I add you because your insights, encouragement, and our rapport put you on par with the above people. Your sharing shows up all over this work. I look forward to reading and hearing your inspiring messages on your blog.

A special thanks goes to **Angelina Sufiyanova** of *Angelinaville Design* for the cover of the book. Thank you for your work and for staying so connected to the project. Special thanks also to my youngest daughter, **Chelsea McKnight,** for hanging in there to assist with the

IF YOU CAN'T CALM THE WATERS, LEARN TO RIDE THE WAVES

Clifton Anthony McKnight

final edit and for providing some magnificent graphics and encouragement.

There are my love circles, family and friends and co-workers, past and present, fellow adventurers in this journey. While you are too many to name, I think that it is appropriate to highlight the magnificent gifts of my most immediate circle beginning with my wife, Michele. My love, our Yin Yang, keep life interesting and adventuresome. To my gifts from God, my daughters Courtney and Chelsea, oh what joy, love, and support I experience because of you.

To my mother, Mary McKnight-Taylor, whose depth of love, intellect, and belief in me shows no bounds, brother Stephen, who I pray continues the path of life with me, and my niece, Tammy, who along with her "Poohdie bear" brought my granddaughter Tyranni Danielle into the world, thanks for your encouragement. I look forward to watching you grow.

I also thank my aunt Thelma Baylor and, posthumously, my Aunt Thelma Minion and step-father William Roscoe Taylor for their wisdom, resilience, and fight. You are and have been wonderful models. Brief interactions and shows of love and support from family in Kingston and New York, NY as well as a visit to Gastonia, North Carolina, fed my soul. To my father, Stephen Charles McKnight Sr, who entered my life that I may come to understand some of my tendencies, including my entrepreneural spirit.

To my cousin, Devron, who in recent years has reached to me because of his concern for my health and

IF YOU CAN'T CALM THE WATERS, LEARN TO RIDE THE WAVES

Clifton Anthony McKnight

wellbeing, keep rolling, keep believing. Cousin Michelle Caldwell, so many times you stepped in and provided a bright light. I send prayers of brighteness to you, too. Carlton and Dorothy Burke, Aunt Louise Forrester and Aunt Cynthia Tracy, Aunt Joy and Cloyd McLennon, thank you for the models you have been and the interest in this work. To my sister-in-law, Carla Milan, thanks for adding your perspective and support to the household. To the entire Burke, Forrester clan who really show the beauty of extended family.

My thanks continue, and it is still only the very tip of the iceberg, less than a scratch on the surface. Please refer to the continued acknowledgements at the conclusion of this book. Remember each conclusion ushers in a new beginning.

To Donald and Mona Williams and their daughters, Dreka and Diedre and to the Unity Christian Fellowship. You are true to Ghandi's edict to "Be the change that you want to see in the world."

To my former neighbors Will and Rise' Jones who even visited me in South Dakota, I appreciate you. You always bring joy, wisdom, and on many occasions, delicious homemade cake. Keep touching lives in your wonderfully comfortable way. To our extended family, Jon and Jan Mangana, Adam and Sophy, Josh and Morgan. When you travel as long and far as we, there is a joy that must be counted, again and again.

To Sandra Glover, some of your thoughts are reflected in this book and more of your spirit. To James Glover and young Jameson seizing the moment and

IF YOU CAN'T CALM THE WATERS, LEARN TO RIDE THE WAVES

Clifton Anthony McKnight

stepping into tomorrow and Yvonne Holmes and Patricia Phipps "you wild and crazy guys" for more laughter and to my brand of the Cosby family, Leo and Leslie, Jennifer, Brandon, Jessica, for living fully, laughing, loving, and sharing.

To my fellow counseling faculty and their families, past and present, to the rest of my Montgomery College (MC) family--faculty, staff, administrators, and students, thank you for your support, for the sabbatical that helped provide the space for this to happen, and the genuine collegiality which is rare, indeed. To the legacy of Harry Harden, to my oasis in the desert in the form of Denise, Simmons Graves, Ever Grier, Gail Wright, Margo Woodward Barnett, and the more than 70 new hires that joined MC along with me. To the positive energy of Nancy Hicks and the can-do attitude of Tonya Harris. To Percy Thomas and Sharon Bowen, you have made a difference.

To the students and employees of Montgomery College, Coppin State University, and Morehouse College, thank you for teaching me. Traveling from across the globe or reaching above your circumstances accepting and expanding your networks, you are ready for the world.

To the employees past, present, and future of the Maryland-National Capital Park and Planning Commission who provide a green space and a fun place for us to re-create ourselves, in order for the world to work, we need you to continue what you do. Special nods go to Trudye Johnson, Luanne Bowles, Bonnie King,

IF YOU CAN'T CALM THE WATERS, LEARN TO RIDE THE WAVES
Clifton Anthony McKnight

Gene Giddens, Mary Ellen Venzke, Judy Cohall, Ronnie Gathers, Fred Johnson and "Butch the poet," to name a few. The world is better because of you, much, much better. To Montgomery County Government, kudos for seeking continuous improvement.

To Forrest Toms, thinker, changemaker, and strategist. Clinita Ford, Educational leader and trailblazer, you have a legacy. To the late Veronica Moorish, to Benelle Rebelle, Chuck Knauer, Dave Ellis, Stan Lankowitz, Larry David, and the College Survival team, the ripple effect is so real.

To Jan Thompson and your bright talented daughters, thanks for friendship and parties. Michele and I still think of you whenever "Ring my bell" comes on.

To the Spencers/Suttons and my many networking families, including the Catletts, the Joines and the Bowies and their lines, that year glimmering over the horizon is here and it has been a more joyful ride because of you. And a specific thanks goes to Jon and Jan Mangana who showed me the way to self help and inspirational works of greats like Napoleon Hill, Earl Nightingale, Og Mandino and David Schwartz, Les Brown, W. Clement Stone, Ben Sweetland and Shad Helmstetter. These greats paved the way for me to find Stephen Covey, Anthony Robbins, Jim Rohn, Wayne Dyer, Brian Tracy, Florence Scoval Shinn, and Jack Canfield. You could say Amway even prepared me for Oprah and the O Magazine.

Special thanks to Harry and U. S. "Sam"Williams AND FAMILY for embacing and encouraging me. Harry

IF YOU CAN'T CALM THE WATERS, LEARN TO RIDE THE WAVES

Clifton Anthony McKnight

planted the seed for this book by suggesting that I keep a folder entitled "Bestseller" many moons ago.

The acknowledgements go on because the continuum is ever present to me. The Wells Family and the families of Charlottesville Virginia thank you for taking in the new guy in town. Frank (Tank) and TJ still in touch today. Reverend and Mrs Mitchell, Young Life and Camp Faith, you all had a hand in my spiritual development.

To the LDS who live service, and Shane and Carlyn Thatcher and family and the Odalhans formerly of South Dakota who reached out to us, thank you. To the Bahai faith whose primary tenets are the unity of all mankind and the equality of men and women. Special thanks to Harry, Shiela Smith, and family as well as Susan and Fitz Weiss and family, and the Magnivito's for bringing a little home living to us when we lived in South Dakota. Thanks to Shirley and Butch Conrad for babysitting the girls so that Michele and I could have our hot tub in the snow experience. To Karen Marie Erickson, presenter extrordinaire and friend.

To my teachers, coaches, and friends from high school and college, some of the life lessons and fond thoughts that contribute to my state in writing this book come from you. To my champion teachers in school and college, thank you for taking a job and making it into a doorway of possibility. Of particular note are the late Dr. Charles D. Sanders of Coppin State University, and Dr. Anna Grant, Dr. Gabriel Hubert, and Dr. Ida Rousseau of Morehouse College. I am grateful for fanning the flame

How to Succeed in Turbulent Times

IF YOU CAN'T CALM THE WATERS, LEARN TO RIDE THE WAVES
Clifton Anthony McKnight

of confidence, social responsibility, and possibility in my spirit.

Continued great props go to MOREHOUSE College for the standards of Benjamin E. Mays and the legacy of Martin luther King, Maynard Jackson, Andrew Young, Spike Lee, Bill Nunn, Samel Jackson, and for Lonnie King and Carlton Molette. Shout outs to the Robert Hall crew of 1970, to the student-athletes who often balance family, work, classes, and practice. To Spelman College and the entire Atlanta University Center.

Thanks to Serena, my daughter's dear friend, passerby Ms. Johnson, Virginia police and EMTs who came to my family's and my aid when we had a car accident and to Deana who reached out to assist me in the Blooms Supermarket when I got a little wobbly. Big thanks to Ian Grant whose light heart and keen skill make giving blood manageable. I acknowlege you, you who extend a hand a smile or a kind word. You start the ripple so others can catch the wave. To Create Space and to 21st century technology for making access feasible. These may be turbulent times, but they are truly times of great possibility as well.

To Cancer survivors, fighters, and their loved ones, I say "Live with cancer? Yes we can sir!" Live now, and you continue to live long after you're gone.

Way too many others whose names do not grace these pages maintain space in my heart. Thanks to all of you who focus on building bridges over building walls. So, you see, when you bring it all together, with such

How to Succeed in Turbulent Times

IF YOU CAN'T CALM THE WATERS, LEARN TO RIDE THE WAVES

Clifton Anthony McKnight

abundant gifts, I must first thank God.

How to Succeed in Turbulent Times

IF YOU CAN'T CALM THE WATERS, LEARN TO RIDE THE WAVES
Clifton Anthony McKnight

About the Author

Inspired by the magnificent legacies of the educators of his past as well as by his own mother, Dr. Mary McKnight-Taylor, Clif McKnight, M.Ed, became an educator. He went on to conduct and facilitate workshops around the country. For over 20 years, Clif has been a keynote speaker. He is Founder and President of MotiVision Inc. and Quantum Success Systems in Maryland. He is also a Professor and Counselor at Montgomery College, Rockville, Md.

Clif also served as an educational consultant dedicated to assisting educators in the U.S. and Canada to help students succeed through first year seminar courses. His interest in supporting students was fed when he himself was a high school student of the federally funded Upward Bound program, a Trio program in Baltimore City. As life would have it, Clif later became Director of Talent Search, another Trio program in Baltimore City. Mr. McKnight asserts that the interconnection of all things provides a loop of wonderful opportunities to serve and be served.

Clifton graduated from Morehouse College in Atlanta Ga., and went on to obtain his M.Ed. from Coppin State College (Now University). Clifton has been married to Michele McKnight for 30 plus years. Clif and Michele have been blessed with two bright, talented, energetic, and creative daughters, Courtney and Chelsea McKnight (They take after their father... okay, they hail from the collective gene pool [smile]).

How to Succeed in Turbulent Times

IF YOU CAN'T CALM THE WATERS, LEARN TO RIDE THE WAVES

Clifton Anthony McKnight

Keep an eye out for the Spanish version of this book and Clifton's other works, scheduled for release in 2012.

SI NO PUEDES CALMAR LAS AGUAS, APRENDE A CORRER LAS OLAS". Como Tener Exito En Los Tiempos Mas Dificiles

QUANTUM SUCCESS WILL OF FORTUNE - Unleash Your Unlimited Potential also on audio

SOUL FOOD FOR THE CHICKEN

How to Succeed in Turbulent Times

<u>IF YOU CAN'T CALM THE WATERS, LEARN TO RIDE THE WAVES</u>

Clifton Anthony McKnight

Visit www.motivision.net or www.cliftonmcknight.wordpress.com for more information and a little inspiration today.

Students, be sure to visit

www.professormcknight.blogspot.com

To Book Clif, call 301-694-7117 or email **cliftonmcknight@motivision.net**

How to Succeed in Turbulent Times

Made in the USA
Middletown, DE
08 May 2025

75225819R00116